LIBRARY USE

A HANDBOOK FOR PSYCHOLOGY

SECOND EDITION

Jeffrey G. Reed and Pam M. Baxter

American Psychological Association
Washington, DC

Published by the
American Psychological Association
Washington, DC

Copies may be ordered from
APA Order Department
P.O. Box 2710
Hyattsville, MD 20784

Cover Design: Michael David Brown, Rockville, MD
Composition and Printing: York Graphic Services, Inc., York, PA
Technical Editing and Production Coordination: Susan Bedford

Library of Congress Cataloging-in-Publication Data

Reed, Jeffrey G., 1948–
   Library use: a handbook for psychology/Jeffrey G. Reed and Pam M. Baxter.—2nd ed.
      p.   cm.
   Includes bibliographical references and index.
   ISBN 1-55798-144-2 (acid-free paper): $19.95
      1. Psychological literature   2. Psychology—Library resources.
   3. Psychology—Research.   I. Baxter, Pam M., 1955–
   II. Title.
      [DNLM: 1. Libraries—handbooks.   2. Psychology—handbooks.
   3. Reference Books—bibliography.   4. Research—methods—
   handbooks.
   BF 76.8 R324L]
   BF76.8.R43   1991
   025.5′6′02415—dc20
   DNLM/DLC
   for Library of Congress   91-31704
                                                                   CIP

Printed in the United States of America
First Printing

Contents

Preface

In writing this new edition, we have updated the contents of *Library Use: A Handbook for Psychology* for the 1990s, adding features that will make this book more useful, while retaining the best features of the first edition.

We have included a variety of new sources. *PsycBOOKS*, an index to chapters in books, is discussed in chapter 4. New sources on psychological tests, including *Test Critiques*, were added to chapter 9. The new CD-ROM technology, which allows users to conduct their own computer bibliographic searches using a microcomputer in the library, is discussed in chapter 8. Many new handbooks, encyclopedias, and other specialized sources (e.g., *Handbook of Adolescent Psychology*) have been added to chapter 2 and appendix A. As appendix C, we have included 14 sample topics which may be used by students or instructors as practice exercises in learning about topic selection and library research.

All chapter search topics were evaluated, resulting in the selection of seven new topic examples (e.g., eyewitness testimony, chapter 4). Topics that were retained have been updated with new references and sources (e.g., aging, chapter 7). In chapter 5, we selected a single interdisciplinary topic, stress, to demonstrate the relevance of literature in education, management, sociology, and health sciences to psychology. In each case, the topics selected

- appeal to the interests of many psychology students,
- represent mainstream psychology (not faddish or fringe),
- do not require highly technical or highly specialized knowledge,
- have a body of published literature, and
- should have information available in a typical college library.

Topics were selected from many different areas of psychology. To insure that the reader has some understanding of a sample topic, summaries are generally more extensive than those provided in the first edition. We hope that inclusion of topics such as eating disorders will make the book relevant and useful for students.

As in the first edition, we have relied heavily on figures to illustrate the use of sources. Their number has increased to provide better coverage of tools such as current-awareness publications, book review sources, and directories. New tools, such as *PsychBOOKS* and *Test Critiques*, warranted new figures. Figures are also a good way to convey changes in format, structure, or content of sources discussed in the first edition.

We hope that these and other changes have resulted in a book that is current, useful, and interesting for students of psychology.

Jeffrey G. Reed
Pam M. Baxter

Acknowledgments

Many people have assisted us in the development of the second edition of *Library Use: A Handbook for Psychology*. Ideas for chapter search topics were provided by Susan Astley, Larry Casler, William Deeds, Richard Hudiburg, Donald Kausler, Mary Ann Lahey, Margaret Matlin, Richard Pringle, George Rebok, and Raymond Wolfe.

We are especially indebted to those who shared their time and expertise with us by reviewing portions of the manuscript: William Deeds, Howard Egeth, Priscilla Geahigan, Robert Jordan, Adelaide LaVerdi, Kathy McGowan, Larry Murdock, Lynn Offerman, Richard Pringle, George Rebok, and Charles Thurston.

From the American Psychological Association, Brenda Bryant initiated second edition work; Carolyn Gosling provided information about *PsycLIT, PsycBOOKs,* and other APA publications and services; Mary Lynn Skutley assisted us in manuscript development; and Susan Bedford has been a helpful production editor.

Staff at the following institutions supported our use of their facilities and collections: Indiana University, Indiana University–Purdue University at Indianapolis, Nazareth College of Rochester, Purdue University, Rochester Institute of Technology, St. John Fisher College of Rochester, University of Rochester, and Xerox Corporation. The second author wishes to acknowledge Purdue University for granting a 6-month sabbatical leave to assist in completion of the manuscript.

Many people contributed to the first edition project, which laid the foundation for this revision: Paddy Berson, Monica Brien, Brenda Bryant, Lawrence Casler, Arelene Dempsey, Karen Duffy, Ellen Dykes, K. Della Ferguson, Margaret Matlin, Kathleen McGowan, Jerry Meyer, Paul Olczak, Virginia O'Leary, Mary Joan Parise, David Parish, Lanna Ruddy, Harriet Sleggs, Nancy Smith, and Gregory Trautt. Others from our past did not contribute directly to the project but enabled us to execute it.

Our spouses, Sylvia and Gordon, were extremely supportive throughout this project.

To all of these people, we owe a debt of gratitude for their assistance. Thank you.

Publication Credits

We would like to thank the following publishers and individuals for permission to reprint copyrighted materials, as noted:

American Psychological Association for our Figures 4–A, 4–B, and 4–C from the *Thesaurus of Psychological Index Terms*, 6th edition, 1991; Figure 4–D from *Psychological Abstracts*, Volume 76, December 1989; Figure 4–E from *Psychological Abstracts*, Volume 75, issue 3, March 1988 and the *Psychological Abstracts* annual subject and author indexes to Volume 75, 1988; Figure 4–F from *Psychological Abstracts*, Volume 70, December 1983, and the *Psychological Abstracts Index* for Volume 70, July–December 1983; Figure 4–G from *Cumulated Author Index to Psychological Abstracts, 1981–1983*; Figure 4–I from *Psychological Abstracts*, Volume 60, 1978; Figures 4–J and 4–K from *PsycBOOKS*, 1989; Figure 8–B from *Psychological Abstracts*, Volume 75, issue 6, June 1988, the annual *Subject Index* to Volume 75, 1988, and the *PsycLIT* database; Figure 10–C from the *Directory of the American Psychological Association*, 1989, Volume II; Figure 10–D from *Contemporary Psychology*, Volume 34, issue 10, October 1989; and Table 4–A from *PsycINFO User Manual*, 1987. Reprinted by permission.

Annual Reviews, Inc., for the excerpt reprinted on pages 14–15 from the Preface of *Annual Review of Psychology*, Volume 32, 1981 (M. R. Rosenzweig and L. W. Porter, Editors). Copyright © 1981 by Annual Reviews, Inc. Reprinted by permission.

Basic Books, Inc., for the excerpt reprinted on page 126 from *The Psychology of Everyday Things* by Donald A. Norman. Copyright © 1988 by Donald A. Norman. Reprinted by permission of Basic Books, Inc., a division of HarperCollins Publishers.

Buros Institute of Mental Measurement at the University of Nebraska at Lincoln for our Figure 9–A from the *Tenth Mental Measurements Yearbook*, 1989. Reprinted by permission.

Cambridge University Press, for the excerpt reprinted on page 9 from Robert J. Sternberg's *The Psychologist's Companion*, 2nd edition, 1988. Reprinted by permission.

Infordata International, Inc., for our Figure 7–D from the *Index to U.S. Government Periodicals*, 1983. Reprinted by permission.

Institute for Scientific Information for our Figures 6–A and 6–B from *Social Sciences Citation Index 1989 Annual*, 1989, Volumes 1 and 5; and for Figure 10–A from *Current Contents: Social & Behavioral Sciences*, Volume 22, issue 28, July 9, 1990. Reprinted by permission.

David E. Kieras for an excerpt from his review in *Contemporary Psychology*, October 1989, in our Figure 10–D. Reprinted by permission.

Donald A. Norman for use of his biographical entry in our Figure 10–C, from the *Directory of the American Psychological Association*, 1989, Volume II. Reprinted by permission.

Oryx Press for our Figure 5–A from the *Thesaurus of ERIC Descriptors*, 12th edition, 1990; Figure 5–B from the *Resources in Education Annual Cumulation 1988: Index*, 1989; and Figures 5–D and 5–E from *Current Index to Journals in Education*, Volume 22, issue 5, May 1990. Reprinted by permission from The Oryx Press, 4041 North Central Avenue, Phoenix, AZ 85012.

PRO-ED for our Figure 9–B from *Test Critiques*, Volume III, 1985. Reprinted by permission.

SilverPlatter Information, Inc., for the format of the *PsycLIT* database citation in Figure 8–B. Reprinted by permission.

Sociological Abstracts, Inc., for our Figure 5–J from the *Thesaurus of Sociological Indexing Terms*, 2nd edition, 1989; Figure 5–K from *Sociological Abstracts: Cumulative Subject Index* to Volume 36, 1988; and Figure 5–L from *Sociological Abstracts*, Volume 36, issue 1, April 1988. Copyright © Sociological Abstracts, Inc. Reprinted by permission.

University Microfilms, Inc., for our Figure 10–B from *Dissertation Abstracts International. Part B: The Sciences and Engineering,* Volume 49, issue 12, June 1989. The dissertation titles and abstracts contained here are published with permission of University Microfilms, Inc., publishers of *Dissertation Abstracts International* (copyright © 1989 by University Microfilms, Inc.) and may not be reproduced without their prior permission. Copies of the dissertations may be obtained by addressing your request to University Microfilms Inc., 300 North Zeeb Road, Ann Arbor, MI 48106, or by telephoning (toll-free) 1-800-521-3042.

H. W. Wilson Company for our Figure 5–F from *Education Index*, Volume 38, July 1987–June 1988 cumulation; and Figure 5–G from *Business Periodicals Index*, Volume 32, issue 5, January 1990. Reprinted by permission.

In addition, we have included numerous illustrations from publications in the public domain prepared by the Educational Resources Information Center, U.S. National Library of Medicine, U.S. Government Printing Office, and the U.S. Library of Congress.

1 Introduction: Getting Started

A library is a storehouse of information recorded over the years. Observations, reflections, empirical data, theories, and so forth are continually reported in books, journals, and other forms by researchers in many fields. Some of this knowledge you will examine in your formal education. A variety of important problems and issues will be dealt with in a textbook chapter or two or during several meeting sessions of a course; some prominent topics may involve a whole course. But there is much information to which you will never be exposed in a classroom, and you will find some issues that you must pursue on your own. Your immediate need for information may stem from a research paper that you have to write for which you must use the library.

We have found that most students have little formal training in the use of a library. Typically, a student's experience is limited to a superficial exposure to the card catalog, a periodical index, and the reserve desk to complete assigned class readings. Consequently, when confronted with a topic necessitating more extensive use of the library, many students fail to locate the information needed.

Although faculty members generally recognize students' need to obtain psychological literature, many are hesitant to assume the task of teaching library-use skills. Some faculty members have never had the benefit of such instruction themselves. Often courses on research methods stress the conduct of empirical research and reporting, allowing little time for instruction in library-use skills. Although some faculty tap the resources of the library's staff to teach such skills, these library sessions usually take only one classroom hour, seldom provide hands-on experience, and offer only a glimpse of the resources available. Thus *Library Use: A Handbook for Psychology* was written to bridge the gap between the need that a student embarking on a psychology research project has for information and the information that is available in the college library.

The Audience

This book is intended as an introduction to library research for college students. It will supplement instruction in library research methods provided in the classroom setting. We anticipate that the typical reader will be enrolled in a college course in experimental psychology or research methods or will be engaged in independent study. The book may be used as a supplement to a textbook on research methods and to the *Publication Manual of the American Psychological Association* (American Psychological Association, 1983). It will also be useful to students in other situations involving research projects such as honors papers. Graduate students and faculty may find the information presented about some of the specialized sources to be a useful supplement to their knowledge of bibliographic tools.

Scope and Approach

Library Use concentrates on information sources available in the typical college library (a library of 100,000 to 300,000 volumes serving a college of 2,000 to 5,000 students). It briefly mentions specialized resources important to researchers in particular subfields of psychology that can be found in larger libraries.

We have made few assumptions about a student's library knowledge and library-use skills. The book provides brief background information concerning each type of source discussed and presents a minisearch to illustrate the use of each major source. Numerous figures illustrate the principles and sources discussed.

A Note on Taking Notes

A first step in taking notes is to get a stack of index cards. One suggestion is to use two different sized cards: smaller cards (e.g., 3″ × 5″ or 4″ × 6″) on which to record *bibliographic information* about sources and larger cards (e.g., 5″ × 8″) on which to take notes about the content of the sources.

Bibliographic information enables you to identify and locate a book, article, or other publication. For books, this information includes the name(s) of the author(s) or editor(s), the title, the place of publication, the publisher, the date of publication, and the call number of the book (for more information about the call number, see chapter 3). For articles, full bibliographic information includes the name(s) of the author(s), the article title, the journal name, the year, the volume number, and the page numbers of the article. Become accustomed to recording information as outlined in the American Psychological Association's *Publication Manual.* Record the complete bibliographic information for each source on a separate card. Such recording helps insure accuracy and completeness and saves time later in the research process. Using a separate card for each source allows you to add relevant sources and delete irrelevant sources as needed. This also makes alphabetizing easier when you prepare your reference list for the paper.

In addition, on each index card record the source or reference tool in which you located the information about the article, book, or other publication. This information will be essential if you need an interlibrary loan (see chapter 11).

When you take notes, use a separate card for each important point in a source and clearly identify exact quotations, taking care to record page numbers. Some people simply make photocopies of sources of interest, which can be useful if the exact wording is needed for a quotation. If many sources have been identified, however, photocopying can be very expensive and the volume of information at your disposal may be overwhelming. In taking notes, identify the main points and summarize material in your own words. You must read and understand the author's points and not just copy the text. Campbell, Ballou, and Slade (1990), Sternberg (1988), and Turabian (1976) are a few authors who provide additional suggestions and details on taking notes and writing the paper.

Careful note-taking also helps you avoid inadvertent plagiarism. Plagiarism, a frequent problem in student papers, is theft. "Plagiarism is stealing other people's words and ideas and making them appear to be your own" (Pauk, 1989, p. 379). Therefore, be sure to provide accurate and complete references to the sources of information and ideas contained in your paper. Plagiarism may result in your failing a course or in your expulsion from college. Gibaldi and Achtert (1988) advise that if you have any doubt about whether something constitutes plagiarism, provide a reference.

A Note on Libraries

There is no such thing as a "typical" college library. A library may be large and spacious, small and cramped, comfortable and quiet, or dreary and noisy. Over the years each library has acquired its own collection of materials reflecting interests of the members of that academic community—librarians, faculty, staff, and students. Most importantly, each library has its own organizational quirks and procedures.

Although the actual materials may vary, all libraries contain the same types of materials: reference works, monographs, periodicals, microforms, government publications, audiovisual materials, and so forth. Differences among libraries are largely in the organization of those materials and size of the collection.

The monographic collection consists of those books and series of books that you may borrow from the library. Every library uses some system to organize and identify *monographs*. In most cases this system is a card catalog (see chapter 3).

Serials are publications issued on a regular or an irregular continuing basis. The *Annual Review of Psychology*, published annually as a bound volume, is a *monographic serial*. The *American Psychologist*, a monthly journal, is another type of serial, known as a *periodical*. *Psychological Abstracts* (see chapter 4), although a reference tool indexing psychological literature, is a monthly periodical. Periodicals may be classified and shelved with monographs, or they may be arranged alphabetically by periodical title. How does your library handle serials?

All libraries contain staffs of librarians and library assistants and have similar functional departments, although these departments may have different names. The acquisitions department staff orders materials. The cataloging staff determines where materials should be located. The staff of the serials department handles the mountains of daily, weekly, monthly, and annual journals, indexes, abstracts, and so forth. Reference librarians help users find what they need and provide instruction in library use. Interlibrary-loan staff members locate and obtain copies of materials needed by researchers but unavailable in the library. These people strive to provide a library that supports the community in its search for information.

Explore your library! Find out where materials—card catalog, periodicals, and so forth—are located. Where is the reference department? Is there a special information desk? When can you get assistance if you need it? Some libraries offer brief 15- or 20-minute library tours at the beginning of each year. Take advantage of this offer to get acquainted.

A Note About Reference Librarians

In your search for information, you will probably have contact primarily with the reference staff. Often located in a central reference room, reference materials typically include such things as handbooks, bibliographies, dictionaries, encyclopedias, periodical indexes, and abstracts. These materials usually may not be borrowed from the library.

Conscientious reference librarians will be glad to assist you with your project; their job is to help people use the library effectively. Their specialty is information retrieval, not usually a subject such as physiological psychology, cultural anthropology, or organic chemistry. As far as fields of study are concerned, librarians tend to be generalists rather than specialists. This general background provides them with a good overview of many fields, an understanding of how the fields relate to one another, and an ability to search for information in many ways and many places.

When you ask a librarian for assistance, be specific, complete, and timely about what you want. Requesting a particular index does not tell the librarian what you need, only what you think you need. Your list of search terms, the definition of your topic, or some of the relevant sources you have already identified may clarify your actual need. Pressing librarians into service the day before a paper is due does not give them (or you) time to do a thorough job. Start early, allow yourself plenty of time, and avoid the end-of-semester rush. By so doing, you enable a librarian to give your request more time and consideration.

What This Book Does and Does Not Cover

Library Use: A Handbook for Psychology will inform you about sources of information available in college libraries, how these sources are organized, and how to use these sources. Chapters 2, 3, and 4 provide basic information about the principles of library and source organization; subsequent chapters assume that the reader is already familiar with this information. Through several examples chapter 2 discusses defining and limiting the topic, which for many students is the most difficult part of the literature search process. Chapter 3 concentrates on using the card catalog to establish the presence of monographic materials and finding these materials in the library. Chapter 4 discusses *Psychological Abstracts,* the most important index to psychological journal literature, and *Psyc-BOOKS*, an index to books and book chapters in the discipline.

Chapter 5 covers important indexes in the related areas of education, management, sociology, and medicine. Whereas chapters 4 and 5 concentrate on subject searches, chapter 6 discusses the author/citation search, which begins with a particular key source. No discussion of libraries would be complete without mention of government publications, especially those of the U.S. federal government. These publications are described in chapter 7. Chapter 8 covers the computer bibliographic search, another approach to the information search. Chapter 9 covers sources of information on psychological tests and measures. Chapter 10 presents some important but less basic sources of information: sources for current research, doctoral dissertations, book reviews, and biographical sources. Chapter 11 helps the individual who has exhausted the resources of his or her own library by providing alternative sources such as interlibrary loan. Appendix A lists selected sources not covered elsewhere in this book. The dictionaries, encyclopedias, bibliographics, indexes, and other sources are more specialized and may not be available in your library. Appendix B, designed to be used as a worksheet, provides a step-by-step overview of literature searching. Appendix C contains a selection of topics that students may find useful as they investigate ideas for research papers. Instructors may also find these topics helpful when assigning paper topics requiring literature search skills.

Library Use will not, however, tell you how to organize or write a paper; for such information, see Campbell, Ballou, and Slade (1990); Sternberg (1988); or Turabian (1976). For discussion of the form of a psychology paper, proper reference style, and so forth, consult the American Psychological Association's *Publication Manual* (1983). Nor will this book tell you how to perform research other than that involving library materials. For discussions of approaches to empirical research—designing an experiment, constructing a questionnaire, collecting data, analyzing data, and so forth—consult books on research methods or statistics (e.g., Elmes, Kantowitz, & Roediger, 1989; Kerlinger, 1986; Wood, 1981).

How to Use This Book

At the beginning of the book, you will find a detailed table of contents, which contains a brief outline for each chapter. This table of contents indicates both the materials in and the organization of each chapter. At the beginning of each chapter, you will find the major sources discussed within that chapter listed in the order of their presentation. References to other materials in each discussion are listed at the end of the chapter. Within each chapter, tables and figures are identified by the chapter number and a sequential letter for each particular table or figure. Some parts in the figures are identified with numbers. Rather than being presented in a key to each figure, these parts, or figure elements, are described and explained in the text, and the corresponding element reference numbers appear in boldface in the text. For your convenience, we have included an index to major sources and important terms at the end of the book.

Throughout *Library Use,* we have emphasized that both knowledge of the bibliographic tools in psychology and search strategy are the keys to the successful literature search. The development of plans for systematic gathering of information is illustrated throughout the book within the context of the sources presented. For this reason, *Library Use* is more than a guide to the literature: it is a tool for learning. After you read a chapter, try to use a source about which you have just read. Practice will reinforce your learning.

References

American Psychological Association. (1983). *Publication manual of the American Psychological Association* (3rd ed.). Washington, DC: Author.

Campbell, W. G., Ballou, S. V., & Slade, C. (1990). *Form and style: Theses, reports, term papers* (8th ed.). Boston: Houghton Mifflin.

Elmes, D. G., Kantowitz, B. H., & Roediger, H. L., III (1989). *Research methods in psychology* (3rd ed.). St. Paul, MN: West.

Gibaldi, J., & Achtert, W. S. (1988). *MLA handbook for writers of research papers* (3rd ed.). New York: Modern Language Association.

Kerlinger, F. N. (1986). *Foundations of behavioral research* (3rd ed.). New York: Holt, Rinehart & Winston.

Pauk, W. (1989). *How to study in college* (4th ed.). Boston: Houghton Mifflin.

Sternberg, R. J. (1988). *The psychologist's companion: A guide to scientific writing for students and researchers* (2nd ed.). Cambridge: Cambridge University Press.

Turabian, K. L. (1976). *Student's guide for writing college papers* (3rd ed.). Chicago: University of Chicago Press.

Wood, G. (1981). *Fundamentals of psychological research* (3rd ed.). Boston: Little, Brown.

2 Selecting and Defining the Topic

Writing a paper should be a personally rewarding learning experience. It should involve your learning about the subject, gaining information, evaluating ideas, and examining issues. It should also aid your personal growth and improve your work habits. The final product should give you a sense of accomplishment. In addition, the paper will be read by someone else—a professor, a thesis advisor, or a journal reviewer—who will evaluate it. You will learn through this evaluation process by receiving positive comments as well as feedback for improvement. Achieving both personal and academic success in writing papers requires that you master each step of the writing process while avoiding a number of pitfalls.

Importance of Selecting and Defining a Topic

The first step in a research project is selecting, narrowing, and defining a topic. Success at this stage is essential for a paper of superior quality. Although at times you may have little latitude because
the topic has been assigned, at other times you may have few con-
straints other than paper length. In the latter case, you may find
selecting a topic to be a difficult task. The topic you select should be
interesting, manageable, and appropriate. Although we cannot tell
you what topic to select, in this chapter we will discuss some common mistakes that students make, and we will present some rules
of thumb for selecting, narrowing, and defining a topic.

Pitfalls to Avoid

Numerous mistakes are possible in writing a paper. Some of the
problems listed below have been noted by other authors (e.g., Kennedy, 1979; Pauk, 1989; Sternberg, 1988; Turabian, 1976); others
are observations we have made. By being aware of these problems,
you may be able to avoid them.

Topic too broad. A common mistake is writing a paper on a topic
that is too broad. Although a textbook may cover topics such as
stress, projective personality tests, conflict, or visual illusions in a
few pages and refer to only a few studies, numerous entire books
have also been written about each of these topics. You probably do
not plan to write a book, so you will have to limit the topic. One way
to limit the paper is to set a time and a page restriction. Other ways
of limiting topics are presented later in this chapter. Unless the
topic is well defined, you risk writing a paper that is superficial,
poorly organized, biased, or all three. Narrow your topic!

Abulia. *Webster's Dictionary* defines abulia as an "abnormal lack of
ability to act or make decisions." Students have several common
sources of abulia: (a) Everything appears to be so interesting that
selecting one topic seems impossible. If you find yourself in this
situation, select several interesting topics, assign a number from 1
to 6 to each one, and roll a die. If the decision of chance is not
acceptable, then you really do have a preference. What is it? (b)
Nothing looks interesting enough for a paper. If you feel this way,
ask yourself why you enrolled in the course. Did you find something
interesting at the beginning? If the course is required, ask yourself
what about the course is so important that it is considered essential. (c) You may feel too poorly informed to select a good paper topic.
Then start skimming the textbook, reading in greater detail sections
that are interesting and finding other sources on the topic. Set a
deadline for selecting a topic!

Procrastination. Library research takes time, and there are few
shortcuts. Procrastination lessens your ability to be successful by
limiting your time and dictating concessions in quality. Alsip and
Chezik (1974) review four typical excuses students give for delay-
ing: (a) "I don't have enough time now," (b) "I'm in the wrong place—
it's too noisy or too quiet, etc.," (c) "Other things are more important," and (d) "I'm not in the right mood." Some aspects of library

research—especially getting started and selecting a topic—can be accomplished by a series of small actions and in a series of small timeblocks. For example, finding a relevant book or copying a review article to get started takes only a few minutes in most college libraries. Divide your project into a number of small tasks and prepare a task schedule. Stop wasting time!

Uninteresting topic. You will find maintaining your motivation for a project over a long period of time extremely difficult if you have little enthusiasm when you initiate the project. If you have little interest in a topic, you may be tempted to throw the paper together at the last minute. Such a paper will probably be disorganized, superficial, poorly documented, poorly typed, and unproofread; it will not only be a waste of time, it might also bring a negative reaction from the reader. Start early, explore several alternative topics, then select a topic that can sustain your interest through the ups and downs of research. Pick a topic that interests you!

Inadequate background. Some topics demand extensive knowledge of mathematics, biology, pharmacology, and so forth. Ask yourself the following questions: Do I have the background in the topic area selected to enable me to read and understand the literature on that topic? If not, will I gain the background as the course progresses, or will I have to study it independently? Do I have the time to spend in such independent study? Assess your own background to determine whether you can handle the topic.

Topic too familiar. Sternberg (1988) comments that "The purpose of student papers is for the student to learn something about some topic. It is therefore to the student's advantage to select a topic with which he [or she] is relatively (although not necessarily totally) unfamiliar. Students sometimes seek to optimize safety (or grades) rather than learning, however, choosing a topic with which they are quite familiar" (p. 15). Although selecting an unfamiliar area may result in a more difficult task, some professors react negatively to the practice of writing papers on the same topic for different courses and assume that the student who does so is attempting to slide by with a minimum of effort. Other professors argue that students who do this are cheating themselves by not seeking a broad education. Thus the personal and academic achievement of writing on a topic already too familiar is suspect. Select a topic about which you can learn something new!

Desire to impress the professor. Writing a paper is a way to integrate, evaluate, and organize your learning and to communicate it to another person. Examine your motives for selecting the topic. Attempting to destroy a theory or to impress the professor with your brilliance may backfire. You may not have the time to read enough material to write an earth-shattering paper. Therefore, select a topic about which you yourself wish to learn.

Controversial topic. The goal of most courses in psychology is cognitive or affective growth or both. When dealing with controversy you may be tempted to find and to use uncritically sources that support your own point of view. Yet, as you become more involved with research, you will find that most topics are far more complex than you initially imagined. Such a discovery may lead to self-examination of your values and behaviors. The discovery of complexity, mixed with self-evaluation, may markedly increase the difficulty of your task. It may result in a positive experience if it leads to a paper of superior quality. It may, however, result in a negative experience if the complexity of the topic or your emotional involvement interferes with your completing the project. Turabian (1976) cautions that a controversial topic demands extreme care. The case must be stated clearly and precisely and must be heavily supported with documentation. Unless you have an open mind and a commitment to do thorough work, you would be well-advised to avoid highly controversial topics.

Resources unavailable. Often the statement, "There's nothing on my topic in the library," results from a student's inability to locate available material. There are, however, some areas in which very little has been written. When selecting your topic, make sure there is enough information to write a good paper.

Reliance on secondary sources. Some students find two or three books and proceed to write a paper based on these sources. This activity is not research; it is book reporting. In general, books are secondary sources, summarizing, interpreting, evaluating, and reporting the research and theorizing of others. Although books are usually accurate, an author may inaccurately report or may exclude an important piece of research because of misinterpretation, prejudice, misjudgment, or sloppy scholarship. Several articles (e.g., Bramel & Friend, 1981; Hogan & Schroeder, 1981; Samelson, 1974) have commented on the apparent inaccuracies in a number of authoritative, standard sources. Unless you read the original source, you cannot be certain that your reporting and evaluation are accurate.

Guidelines for Selecting a Topic

Having recounted a list of potential problems and situations to avoid, we now offer positive suggestions for selecting a topic. You should select a topic that meets the following criteria:

- **Interesting:** The topic should be something about which you want to learn.
- **Appropriate:** The topic should be directly relevant to your situation. You should have the background and knowledge to be able to read and understand the materials you encounter.
- **Manageable:** The topic must be sufficiently limited so that you can do a credible job in the time and space available. You will probably need to restrict your topic several times after selecting an initial topic area.
- **Researchable:** The topic should be feasible given the resources available to you.

For other discussions of topic selection, consult such sources as Campbell, Ballou, and Slade (1990), Pauk (1989), Sternberg (1988), or Turabian (1976).

Defining the Topic

A clear, concise *topic definition* is essential for an effective literature search. Such a definition will provide guidelines for evaluating materials and determining their relevance or irrelevance. After spending hours of reading and taking notes on material for your paper, you may be tempted to include unessential information in the paper. Such inclusion may result in a disorganized, poorly focused paper. You can minimize this temptation by effectively defining your topic.

Campbell, Ballou, and Slade (1986) suggest two ways of expressing a topic: (a) as a thesis statement or (b) as a question. For example, the following might be acceptable ways of initially defining a topic concerning occupational stress:

- **Thesis statement:** Occupational stress has a negative effect on interpersonal relations and thus adversely affects job performance in managerial workers.
- **Question:** What is the effect of occupational stress on managerial job performance in situations concerning interpersonal relations?

Either of these ways of expressing the topic might be an acceptable form in your situation. Both of these topic sentences, however, are still fairly broad. What kinds of interpersonal relations—peer relations, supervisor-subordinate relations, and so on—and what kind of job performance will you consider? Exactly what do you mean by occupational stress? Thus you must take the next step and narrow the topic to a more manageable size.

Limiting the Topic

You can narrow a topic several times in several ways. Pauk (1989) suggests that every topic be subjected to three or four significant narrowings to reach a topic of manageable size. The following list, based in part on suggestions of Sternberg (1988), shows a number of dimensions along which a topic may be limited.

Subject population. Age limitation: You may be interested only in a particular age group, for example, infants, adolescents, college students, or retirees. Occupational group limitation: You may be interested only in middle managers, blue-collar workers, secretaries, or military personnel. Racial or ethnic limitation: You may be interested only in African Americans, Native Americans, Spanish-speaking Americans, or Asian Americans.

Theoretical approach. You might limit a clinically oriented study to a behavior-modification approach, a Gestalt approach, or a psychodynamic approach. For a study in human judgment you might select from among a Bayesian, an information-integration, or a policy-capturing approach.

Species restriction. In a learning, comparative, physiological, or ethological study, you might focus your interest on rats, pigeons, chimpanzees, cats, dogs, eels, chickens, or humans.

Research methodology employed. You might limit consideration to only laboratory studies, simulations, field experiments, surveys, interviews, or naturalistic observations. Your reporting might concentrate on studies that involve deception or on those that do not involve deception, on studies that involve a particular piece of psychological equipment, or on studies that employ a particular psychological test.

Content of problem. In an information-processing topic, you might consider only studies of numerical information, those of verbal information, or those of pictorial information. Or you might limit the number of examples and treat these in depth. In a study of perceptual illusions, you might limit yourself to one or two particular illusions.

Limiting a topic depends upon your purpose in writing the paper and upon the area you wish to cover. You might need to limit two different topics in entirely different fashions for different reasons. The way you limit a topic ultimately depends upon making good judgments. But how and where do you begin?

Sources to Get Started

After you have selected and defined a general topic, you are ready to begin the process of narrowing. A good way to figure out how to narrow your topic is to consult several types of general sources to get a feel for the area, an overview of the topic, and a number of subareas or subtopics from which to select. These general sources should also provide relevant and major references for beginning your search. This section discusses three types of general sources: (a) textbooks, (b) handbooks, and (c) annual reviews. To illustrate the use of these sources, we have selected three different topics and will narrow each topic using one of the three sources.

Textbooks. You might begin with your textbook, reading material relevant to your topic several times. This material may span an entire chapter (a hint that the topic is broad and requires considerable limiting), or the material may be covered in a paragraph or two. Check the sources that are cited. Every good textbook should refer to important, relevant sources, providing complete bibliographic information for all major topics covered. With those references, you can start a literature search, using the references provided in those sources to find other materials. If, however, the topic that interests you is not mentioned in your textbook, find another recent textbook that does cover the topic. In the course of gathering this information, you will find phrases that will help you in limiting your topic.

To illustrate topic limitation, we consider a topic popular in developmental psychology, Piaget's theory of child development. In their textbook, *Child Psychology: A Contemporary Viewpoint,* Hetherington and Parke (1986) discuss Piaget's theory in chapters 9 and 16. The discussion in these chapters as well as references to four books by Piaget indicate that this theory of child development is a large topic. Chapter 9, however, covers a more limited area: "Piaget's Cognitive Developmental Theory of Intelligence." Within

TABLE 2–A

Sequential Steps in Limiting a Topic in Developmental Psychology

Stage	Topic Statement
Initial topic	Piaget's theory of child development
1st narrowing	Piaget's cognitive developmental theory of intelligence
2nd narrowing	Cognitive development in the intuitive period
3rd narrowing	Conservation in the intuitive period
4th narrowing	Conservation of number in the intuitive period
5th narrowing	Training conservation in the intuitive period
Final statement	Effectiveness of attempts to stimulate cognitive development in intuitive-period children (age 4–7) through training conservation

that chapter, pages 357 to 364 cover the intuitive period (age 4–7) of a child's development. Although this topic is narrower, we still have much to consider: problems of conservation, transformations, centration, irreversibility, and part–whole relations. Looking at the illustrations, we see that Figure 9–3 mentions tests for conservation of substance, length, number, liquids, and area.

If you were working on this topic, you might, at this point, limit the topic to conservation of number. You might focus on the issue that some researchers have wondered whether training children in conservation strategies can stimulate cognitive growth in other areas. You then might settle on the topic of the "effectiveness of attempts to stimulate cognitive growth in intuitive-period children through training conservation." You have now narrowed your topic by selecting a specific subject population (intuitive-age children), theoretical approach (Piagetian conception of conservation), and problem content (effect of conservation training on other areas of learning). This topic narrowing is summarized in Table 2–A. Finally, the textbook provides several relevant references, which give you a direction in which to start your library research.

Handbooks. If you have already decided on an area you wish to study, you will find a logical second source is a handbook. Most handbooks have several characteristics that make them especially well suited for narrowing a topic and beginning a literature search.

- They provide an authoritative summary of a particular area, including evaluations of theory and research.
- They are written by experts in the field. Although one person sometimes writes a handbook, more commonly one person edits the contributions of a large number of authors, each of whom writes in his or her special area of interest and expertise.
- They are usually written at a level for a beginning graduate student in a particular subfield and are more comprehensive than most textbooks.
- They contain extensive reference lists.

TABLE 2–B

Sequential Steps in Limiting a Topic in Social Psychology: Psychology of Women

Stage	Topic Statement
Initial topic	Women as leaders
1st narrowing	Women's success as leaders
Final statement	Attributes of successful women managers

Be aware, however, that not all subfields of psychology are covered by recent handbooks. In some areas, such as brain biochemistry, human factors in display-control design, and information processing, handbooks can become obsolete very rapidly.

The use of one handbook is illustrated in this section. At the end of this chapter, you will find a selected list of handbooks that might help you begin.

Suppose your topic is women as leaders, a contemporary concern in social psychology, organizational psychology, and psychology of women. One logical starting point is *Stogdill's Handbook of Leadership* (Bass, 1981). When you examine the table of contents (or the subject index), you see that chapter 30, "Women and Leadership," appears to be useful. This 17-page chapter contains references to approximately 200 sources. It also divides the topic of women and leadership into six major areas: societal conditions, male–female differences in leadership potential, male–female differences in leadership style, sex effects contingent on groups and situations, women's success as leaders, and the effectiveness of women leaders. Although you could use these divisions to narrow the topic—you could, for example, pick "women's success as leaders" (section 5)— you would be advised to limit the topic still further because of the large amount of information available. Part 2 of section 5 covers the "attributes of the successful woman manager," which seems to be a good possibility for research. This section contains 14 references, most of which are fairly recent. At the outset, then, the topic appears to be reasonably limited, with some relevant resources. Thus you have limited this topic by your own interest, by subject population (women, managers), and by content of the problem (effective managers). The successive topic limiting may be seen more easily in Table 2–B.

Annual reviews. A third important source of information for defining and limiting a topic is the *Annual Review of Psychology*. The first volume, containing 18 review articles, appeared in 1950. Since then, the annual volumes have included from 15 to 22 articles each year. In recent years, as the field of psychology has expanded, reviews have become more focused and specialized, and new topics have been added. The plan of the *Annual Review* is well summarized in the preface to Volume 32 (1981):

> Each volume is planned to present selective and evaluative reviews of status and recent progress in several main areas of psychology. We do not intend to provide in a single volume an accurate representation of activity in each of the many subfields of psychology: space would not permit this. Rather, we try to follow (and frequently revise) a Master

Plan according to which some topics appear each year, some every other year, and some less frequently. In this way, a few successive volumes, taken together, present an evaluative portrayal of the main recent findings and interpretations as they are viewed by the most expert judges who can be persuaded to contribute their critical and integrative skills to the task. (Rosenzweig & Porter, 1981, p. v)

In addition to areas that are covered frequently as part of the Master Plan, other topics of timely interest have been covered, as well as reviews of developments in psychological research in other countries. A sampling of recent topics includes the following: cognitive science, perception and information, health psychology, hemispheric asymmetry, environmental psychology, psychophysical scaling, human learning and memory, child and adolescent psychotherapy, visual sensitivity, organizational behavior, consumer psychology, social motivation, and attitudes and attitude change.

For illustrative purposes, suppose your topic is the reward effect of direct brain stimulation. Volume 40 of the *Annual Review of Psychology* contains a relevant review by Wise and Rompre (1989), focusing on the role of dopaminergic neurons in reward. The review considers evidence from two approaches to direct brain reward: electrical stimulation and chemical (drug) stimulation. Limiting our topic to electrical stimulation, we could further restrict it to anatomical mapping studies (pp. 197–201) rather than lesion, autoradiographic, or neurochemical studies. Thus, we have narrowed our topic by type of research method (mapping studies), brain stimulation method (electrical), and brain mechanism (dopaminergic neurons). The steps in narrowing this topic are summarized in Table 2–C.

Two notes are important. First, it may be useful to consult multiple annual review volumes for additional references or alternate interpretations. For example, Volume 32 of the *Annual Review of Psychology* contained a related review by Olds and Fobes (1981) on self-stimulation of the brain which we would also check for relevant references. Second, some topics in psychology, such as this one, demand extensive knowledge of other fields (e.g., brain physiology and biochemistry).

TABLE 2–C

Sequential Steps in Limiting a Topic in Physiological Psychology

Stage	Topic Statement
Initial topic	Reward effect of brain stimulation
1st narrowing	Reward effect of direct electrical stimulation of the brain
2nd narrowing	Role of dopaminergic neurons in reward resulting from direct electrical brain stimulation
Final statement	Role of dopaminergic neurons in reward resulting from direct electrical stimulation of the brain as reported in anatomic mapping studies

Nothing should prevent your use of all three of these types of sources. Because each source is selective, presenting only a few of the many available resources, you can expect each to contain a slightly different group of primary source materials. Furthermore, because the sources are written by different authors, they express different points of view.

Selecting Subject-Search Terms

The final preliminary step in doing library research is developing a set of subject terms to be used to search for information. When beginning research in a new area, students often search for information by subject. Most sources, including all of the sources discussed in the following chapters, contain subject indexes. However, indexes are compiled by different people, some by psychologists and others by persons having little detailed knowledge of psychology. As a result, the index of each source will be different and may use a different set of subject-indexing terms.

Determining in advance how a particular topic will be indexed is difficult. For example, in the sample topic on leadership, you might find that some sources list information only under *women managers*, whereas others use only the term *female managers*. Sources may include research under one of the terms *leadership, supervision,* or *management* but not under all three. Because of the complexity of the subject of personality, terms used to describe a successful woman manager might be *characteristics, attributes, traits,* or *styles*.

As a result, you must compile a list of subject-search terms that you could use to locate relevant information on a topic. You should include in this list any synonyms, technical terms, or important aspects of the topic of interest. Later, as you use particular sources, you may modify the list of search terms to match the subject-indexing terms of each source.

Table 2–D contains sample lists of search terms for the three topics illustrated in this chapter. Each list is different in the number of

TABLE 2–D

Initial Lists of Search Terms for Sample Topics

Topic	Search Terms	
Training conservation in children	Conservation (psychology) Intuitive period Teaching conservation Child intelligence	Cognitive development Child development Piaget
Successful women leaders	Women Females Managers Leaders Supervisors	Characteristics Traits Attributes Styles
Self-stimulation of of the brain	Brain stimulation Neural stimulation Mapping Dopaminergic neurons Electrical stimulation	Opiate receptors Dopamine Neurochemistry Reward

terms, the technicality of terms, and the number of synonyms. In every search, these differences will reflect the particular character of the research topic.

Summary Steps in Defining a Topic

The following is a brief review of six general steps in getting started. A different sequence may better suit your style, but at some point, each process requires attention.

- Select a general topic, being as specific as possible.
- Define the topic as a statement or as a question.
- Get an overview of the topic by reading the textbook, a handbook, an annual review chapter, or all three.
- Limit the topic to a manageable size.
- Redefine the narrowed topic.
- Devise a list of possible search terms.

You are now ready to start consulting the primary sources you have already located and to begin searching for additional relevant references.

Selected Handbooks

This list of handbooks is intended to be illustrative rather than exhaustive. The sources are grouped by general area. All of the handbooks mentioned here contain extensive lists of references. A few handbooks are a bit old, and, to the extent that they cover rapidly changing fields, you must use them with care.

General Sources

Atkinson, R. C., Herrnstein, R. J., Lindzey, G., & Luce, R. D. (Eds.). (1988). *Stevens' handbook of experimental psychology* (2nd ed., Vols. 1–2). New York: Wiley.

Twenty-seven chapters by over forty contributors. Volume 1 is titled *Perception and Motivation*, and Volume 2 covers *Learning and Cognition*. This is a revision of Stevens' classic 1951 handbook.

Kling, J. W., et al. (1971). *Woodworth and Schlossberg's experimental psychology* (3rd ed.). New York: Holt, Rinehart & Winston.

Twenty-one chapters, 1,100 pages, 100-page bibliography. This classic is geared toward the advanced undergraduate or first-year graduate student. The original edition was published in 1938 and was intended as a textbook. Its authoritativeness and comprehensiveness make it usable as a handbook, although it is now severely dated. It covers such topics as psychophysics; chemical senses; color vision; and transfer, inference, and forgetting.

Wolman, B. B. (Ed.). (1973). *Handbook of general psychology*. Englewood Cliffs, NJ: Prentice-Hall.

Forty-five chapters, 950+ pages, multiple authors. Chapters include "Theories of Intelligence" by J. P. Guilford, "Theories of Motivation" by K. B. Madsen, and "Structured Personality Assessment" by D. N. Jackson.

Learning, Motivation, and Sensory Processes

Boff, K. R., Kaufman, L., & Thomas, J. P. (Eds.). (1986). *Handbook of perception and human performance* (Vols. 1–2). New York: Wiley.

A total of 45 chapters by 66 contributors. Volume 1 is titled *Sensory Processes and Perception* and Volume 2 *Cognitive Processes and Performance.*

Carterette, E. C., & Friedman, M. (Eds.). (1973–1978). *Handbook of perception* (10 vols.). New York: Academic Press.

Ten volumes, multiple authors. Volumes include the following: *I. Historical and Philosophical Roots of Perception; III. Biology of Perceptual Systems; V. Seeing; X. Perceptual Ecology.*

Psychology of learning and motivation: Advances in research and theory. (1967–present, Vols. 1+). New York: Academic Press.

Published annually, multiple authors. This handbook may be seen as a companion to the *Annual Review of Psychology,* with a narrower range of topics.

University of Nebraska, Department of Psychology. (1953–present). *Current theory and research in motivation, a symposium.* (Vol. 1+). Lincoln, NE: University of Nebraska Press.

Commonly known as *Nebraska Symposium on Motivation;* published annually. Strictly speaking, this is not a handbook; however, important articles represent the state of the art at the time of their publication. For many years, this symposium has played a key role in the development of motivational psychology. In recent years, volumes have focused on a broad theme: for example, "Response Structure and Organization," "Psychology and Gender," and "Alcohol and Addictive Behavior."

Developmental, Personality, and Social

Abelson, R. P., Aronson, E., McGuire, W. J., Newcomb, T. M., Rosenberg, M. J., & Tannenbaum, P. H. (Eds.). (1968). *Theories of cognitive consistency: A sourcebook.* Chicago: Rand McNally.

Eighty-four chapters, 800+ pages. Approaches covered include balance theory (F. Heider), conflict theory (K. Lewin), dissonance theory (L. Festinger), and congruity theory (C. E. Osgood & P. M. Tannenbaum). Although dated, the book provides an excellent review of cognitive consistency theories.

Birren, J. E., & Schaie, K. W. (Eds.). (1990). *Handbook of the psychology of aging* (3rd ed.). New York: Van Nostrand Reinhold.

Twenty-eight chapters cover the influences on and consequences of individual, social, and developmental aspects of aging.

Knutson, J. N. (Ed). (1973). *Handbook of political psychology.* San Francisco: Jossey-Bass.

Sixteen chapters, including "Political Attitudes," Political Socialization," and "Experimental Research."

Lindzey, G., & Aronson, E. (Eds.). (1985). *Handbook of social psychology* (3rd ed., Vols. 1–2). New York: Random House.

A classic and excellent reference contained in 30 chapters. Volume I is titled *Theory and Method,* and Volume II is *Special Fields and Applications.*

Mussen, P. H. (Ed.). (1983). *Handbook of child psychology* (4th ed.). New York: Wiley.

Four volumes, 47 chapters, more than 75 contributing authors. Volumes: *I. History, Theory and Methods* (W. Kessen, Ed.); *II. Infancy and Developmental Psychology* (J. Campos & M. Haith, Eds.); *III. Cognitive Development* (J. Flavell & E. Markman, Eds.); *IV. Socialization, Personality and Social Development* (E. M. Hetherington, Ed.).

Osofsky, J. D. (Ed.). (1987). *Handbook of infant development.* (2nd ed.). New York: Wiley.

Over 1,000 pages, 27 chapters by 43 contributors, including T. Field, J. Kagan, and R. Plomin. The first two years of human development are covered in chapters on learning and memory, family interaction, behavioral genetics, and mental health.

Pervin, L. A. (Ed.). (1990). *Handbook of personality: Theory and research.* New York: Guilford Press.

Twenty-seven chapters cover theoretical approaches to personality, biological and social aspects, psychopathology, and individual differences.

Van Hasselt, V. B., & Hersen, M. (Eds.). (1987). *Handbook of adolescent psychology.* New York: Pergamon Press.

Twenty-five chapters by 42 contributors. Chapters include "Adolescent Sexuality," "Family and Environment," "Substance Abuse in Adolescence," and "Adolescent Culture and Subculture."

Operant Behavior

Gambrill, E. D. (1977). *Behavior modification: A handbook of assessment, intervention and evaluation.* San Francisco: Jossey-Bass.

Twenty-three chapters, 1,000+ pages. Chapters include "Assessment," "Intervention Plans," "Anxiety Reduction," "Drug Abuse," "Depression," "Educational Settings," and "Ethics."

Honig, W. K., & Staddon, J. E. R. (Eds.). (1977). *Handbook of operant behavior.* Englewood Cliffs, NJ: Prentice-Hall.

Progress in behavior modification. (1975–present, Vols. 1+). New York: Academic Press.

Published annually, multiple authors. The preface to Volume 1 describes this handbook as a "multidisciplinary serial publication encompassing the contributions of psychology, psychiatry, social work, speech therapy, education, and rehabilitation."

Clinical, Counseling, and Industrial–Organizational

Adams, H. E., & Sutker, P. B. (Eds.). (1984). *Comprehensive handbook of psychopathology*. New York: Plenum Press.

Thirty-four chapters by 58 authors, 1,000+ pages. Some chapters cover broad topics in psychopathology, such as "Psychopathology and Genetics" and "Abnormal Behavior in Cultural Context." Others discuss broad classes of disorders, such as schizophrenias, affective disorders, and autism.

Dunnette, M. D., & Hough, L. M. (Eds.). (1990–). *Handbook of industrial and organizational psychology* (2nd ed.). Palo Alto, CA: Consulting Psychologists Press.

To be completed in four volumes. Chapters in Volume 1 focus on theory and research methods and include "Motivation Theory and Industrial and Organizational Psychology," "Judgment and Decision-making Theory," and "Item Response Theory." Volume 2 focuses on behavior and characteristics of individuals in organizations, covering job analysis, personnel recruitment, placement, and testing and evaluation.

Matson, J. L., & Mulick, J. A. (Eds.). (1983). *Handbook of mental retardation*. New York: Pergamon Press.

Forty chapters by 66 contributors discuss classification, assessment, rehabilitation, treatment, and social issues concerned with mental retardation syndromes.

Rie, H. E., & Rie, E. D. (Eds.). (1979). *Handbook of minimal brain dysfunctions: A critical view*. New York: Wiley.

Twenty-seven chapters, 31 contributors. Chapters include "Concept of MBD," "Determinants of MBD," "Evaluation of MBD," and "Intervention."

Struening, E. L., & Guttentag, M. (Eds.). (1975). *Handbook of evaluation research*. Beverly Hills, CA: Sage.

Chapters cover a range of issues, including those of political influences, design of evaluation studies, and data analysis. Originally published in two volumes, a one-volume abridged version with updated bibliographic references was published in 1983.

Woody, R. H. (Ed.). (1980). *Encyclopedia of clinical assessment*. San Francisco: Jossey-Bass.

Two volumes, 91 chapters, 110 authors. Chapters include "Academic Learning Problems," "Affective Guilt States," "Aggression," "Altruism," "Ambiguity Tolerance," and "Antisocial Personality."

References

Alsip, J. E., & Chezik, D. D. (1974). *Research guide in psychology*. Morristown, NJ: General Learning Press.

Bass, B. M. (1981). *Stogdill's handbook of leadership: A survey of theory and research* (2nd ed.). New York: Free Press.

Bramel, D., & Friend, R. (1981). Hawthorne, the myth of the docile worker, and class bias in psychology. *American Psychologist, 36,* 867–878.

Campbell, W. G., Ballou, S. V., & Slade, C. (1986). *Form and style: Theses, reports, term papers* (7th ed.). Boston: Houghton Mifflin.

Campbell, W. G., Ballou. S. V., & Slade, C. (1990). *Form and style: Theses, reports, term papers* (8th ed.). Boston: Houghton Mifflin.

Hetherington, E. M., & Parke, R. D. (1986). *Child psychology: A contemporary viewpoint* (3rd ed.). New York: McGraw-Hill.

Hogan, R., & Schroeder, D. (1981, July). Critique: Seven biases in psychology. *Psychology Today,* pp. 8–14.

Kennedy, J. R. (1979). *Library research guide to education: Illustrated search strategies and sources.* Ann Arbor, MI: Pierian Press.

Olds, M. E., & Fobes, J. L. (1981). The central basis of motivation: Intracranial self-stimulation studies. *Annual Review of Psychology, 32,* 523–574.

Pauk, W. (1989). *How to study in college* (4th ed.). Boston: Houghton Mifflin.

Rosenzweig, M. R., & Porter, L. W. (Eds.). (1981). *Annual Review of Psychology,* Vol. 32. Palo Alto, CA: Annual Reviews, Inc.

Samelson, F. (1974). History, origin myth, and ideology: "Discovery" of social psychology. *Journal of the Theory of Social Behavior, 4,* 217–231.

Sternberg, R. J. (1988). *The psychologist's companion: A guide to scientific writing for students and researchers* (2nd ed.). Cambridge: Cambridge University Press.

Turabian, K. L. (1976). *Student's guide for writing college papers* (3rd ed.). Chicago: University of Chicago Press.

Wise, R. A., & Rompre, P. O. (1989). Brain dopamine and reward. *Annual Review of Psychology, 40,* 191–225.

3 Locating a Book

Sources Discussed
Library Card Catalog
Library of Congress, Subject Cataloging Division. (1988–present). *Library of Congress subject headings.* Washington, DC: Library of Congress. Annual, with previous editions published irregularly.

This chapter discusses procedures for identifying and locating monographs (books) in the library. Monographs appear in many formats: single-volume books (e.g., *Library Use*), multiple-volume sets (e.g., *Handbook of Perception*), annual series (e.g., *Annual Review of Psychology*), and so forth. They may contain reviews of literature and extensive bibliographies. Some books contain important new theoretical approaches; others contain original empirical contributions. However, books may be limited in several ways. They may present only one author's point of view or only his or her research. Because writing and publishing a book is a time-consuming process, it may not contain the most recent research. Hence, although books may provide important background for your literature reviews, they should be only part of your research. You will also need to locate journals (discussed in chapters 4, 5, and 6), in which most research reports are published.

This chapter discusses the card catalog, an index to monographs contained in a library. We also discuss online computerized book catalogs, an alternative to the traditional card catalog that is available in some libraries.

Chapter Example: Intelligence

Intelligence has long been a subject of interest to students, scholars, and practitioners. Many aspects of intelligence could be discussed.

One such topic is intelligence testing. Early work by Alfred Binet has had a significant impact on methods of intelligence measurement. Binet believed that intellect is composed of judgment, common sense, initiative, and adaptation ability and is distinct from acquired information. Working with Theophile Simon, he developed the Binet–Simon Scale, which attempted to measure intelligence by assessing a person's success in completing a series of complex tasks which were thought to reflect aspects of intelligence (Binet & Simon, 1916). Lewis Terman's (1916) Stanford Revision of the Binet–Simon Scale, typically referred to as the Stanford–Binet, a translation and adaptation of the tasks, is one of the most influential tests available today and is the yardstick against which all other tests of intelligence are measured. Succeeding work led to the development of paper-and-pencil group tests such as the Cognitive Abilities Test (Thorndike & Hagen, 1978). Over the years, measures such as these have been used in the assessment of academic ability by school psychologists, for personnel selection in industry, and for selection and placement by the military.

Controversy has been associated with intelligence tests for many years. For example, what is the utility of infant tests of intelligence given that their predictive validity appears to be very low (Lewis, 1973)? The nature–nurture controversy—that is, to what extent is intelligence determined by heredity, as opposed to the environment to which one is exposed—has received much attention. This has led to further questions regarding racial differences in intelligence and the extent to which it may be possible to modify intelligence through intervention programs such as Head Start (e.g., Jensen, 1969; Kamin, 1974). Because cultures encourage different ways of behaving and different abilities, what is viewed as intelligent in one culture is not necessarily viewed the same way in all cultures. Thus, a test designed for one culture is not necessarily valid for another, and measurement methods must be adjusted (Brislin, Lonner, & Thorndike, 1974).

The most fundamental questions, however, revolve around the definition and understanding of intelligence—what is it? Over the years, many theories have been developed. Charles Spearman (1927) attempted to describe intelligence in terms of a single general factor, "g." Louis Thurstone (1938) suggested the existence of seven primary mental abilities. J. P. Guilford (1967) proposed over 100 factors of intelligence in his structure of intellect model. Raymond Cattell (1971) argued for two general aspects of intelligence: fluid and crystallized ability. Each of these approaches, however, seems to have limitations.

A current approach to understanding intelligence is Robert Sternberg's Triarchic Theory. He suggests that "the intelligent person is not someone who merely does well on a test or in the classroom, but one who can use his or her mind to fullest advantage in all the various transactions of everyday life" (Sternberg, 1988, xiii). He postulates three mental processes: meta-components, perfor-

TABLE 3–A

Alphabetical Orderings of Selected Authors, Titles, and Subjects of Books

Author	Title	Subject
Adorno, T. W.	*Basic Behavioral Statistics*	Emotions
Allport, G. W.	*Behavior and Psychological Man*	Environment
Anastasi, A.	*Behavior Therapy*	Evolution
Anderson, N. H.	*The Behavioral Sciences Today*	Experiments
Aronson, E.	*Being Mentally Ill*	Fantasy
Bandura, A.	*Beyond Burnout*	Fear

mance components, and knowledge-acquisition components. These three processes take place within an environmental context to which the individual relates through adaptation, selection, and shaping. This is proposed as an integrated theory that examines the components of intelligence, the relation of components to experience, and the impact of intelligence on the individual's experience of the external world context.

This chapter focuses on the topic of human intelligence to illustrate the search for monographs. Using Sternberg's (1988) book as a starting point, we will search for other monographs which may help us to understand what human intelligence is.

A Word About Library Catalogs

Until recently, most libraries maintained standard card catalogs: large cabinets in which cards representing their books were filed. Increasingly, libraries are using automated methods to make information about their book collections available to their users, meaning that the familiar card catalog cabinets are being supplemented or replaced by computer terminals. Some libraries use card catalogs exclusively, some use only the computerized approach to their book collections, and some use a combination of the two. Because a card catalog remains in many college libraries, this is where our discussion will begin. Use of the card catalog and its organization will, in many cases, enhance use of an automated catalog, should your library use one.

Card Catalog

We can begin to identify other books on the nature, components, and manifestation of intelligence by locating Sternberg's book in the library. Every library uses some system to organize its hundreds of thousands of books. Most libraries arrange books on the shelf by codes known as *call numbers*, which are printed on the spine (bound end) of the book. To find the number of Sternberg's book, we need to use an index to those call numbers. For most libraries, that index is the card catalog.

You are probably familiar with three basic types of indexes. In author indexes information is arranged in alphabetical order by the last name of the person who wrote a book or paper. In title indexes material is arranged alphabetically by title. In subject indexes, books are listed alphabetically by general topic and, within the general topic, alphabetically by subtopic. Table 3–A illustrates each of these types of indexes. Card catalogs contain entries of all three types for each book in the library. Some libraries group all three types of indexes together in a single alphabetical order (a dictionary catalog). Other libraries separate the different types of index entries (divided catalogs); for example, a library may have one catalog combining the author and title indexes (author/title catalog) and a separate catalog that contains the subject index (subject catalog). It is important to remember that a catalog is a finding tool to books, not to individual chapters contained within books. For access to book chapters, see the discussion of *PsycBOOKS* in Chapter 4 of this volume.

When looking for a book by a particular author, you must start with the *author catalog*. With the author selected for illustration, you would therefore start by searching for "Sternberg, Robert J." Cards in the catalog are filed alphabetically by the top line of each card, in this case, by the author's last name (surname), then by the first name and middle initial, if any. If the top lines of several author cards are identical (indicating several books by the same author), cards are ordered alphabetically by the title, which usually appears on the second line. Books with more than three authors may have the title on the top line.[1] Each catalog card provides the same types of information about books in the same relative position on the card.

When you go to the catalog, you should find a card that looks like the picture of the 3″ × 5″ catalog card in Figure 3–A. In that figure, the author, Robert J. Sternberg, is listed at the top of the card (1), and the rest of the bibliographic information follows. The title of Sternberg's book is *The Triarchic Mind: A New Theory of Human Intelligence* (2). The book was published in New York, New York (3) by Viking (4) in 1988 (5). The lines that follow provide a physical description of the book (6): The book has 13 prefatory pages and 354 pages of text, contains illustrations, is approximately 25 centimeters (9.8 inches) tall, includes a bibliography on pages 339 through 346, and has an index. The International Standard Book Number (ISBN) (7), is a unique number assigned by the book's publisher and identifies this edition of the book.

Below the descriptive information on the card are the *tracings* (8), which inform the librarian and the library user how this particular

---

[1]There are numerous exceptions to general rules regarding libraries; the catalog contains many. Four common problems are illustrated here. Although APA publication style uses the author's first and middle initials in references, most libraries make entries under the author's full name, if it is known. Thus a book by Adam Smith would be cited as "Smith, A." in an APA publication; it would be filed in the card catalog under "Smith, Adam." This distinction is particularly important with authors who have common surnames, for example, Johnson, Jones, or Smith.

In many libraries, names beginning with M', Mc, and Mac are ordered together as if all were spelled "Mac." The following list illustrates card catalog ordering of several names: MacBride, McDowell, MacGregor, M'Intosh, Mack, Macmillian, McShane.

Separate entries may be made for an author and a subject that appear to be the same. For example, books by Freud would appear in the author catalog under "Freud, Sigmund." Books about him or about his writings would be entered in the subject catalog (or, in a combined catalog, after all books written by him) under the all-uppercase subject heading, FREUD, SIGMUND.

If a book title begins with an article (i.e., *a, an,* or *the*), librarians overlook this article when alphabetizing titles in the card catalog. For example, *The Origin of Species* would be filed alphabetically under "Origin of species."

FIGURE 3–A

Card-catalog author (main entry) cards for Robert J. Sternberg's (1988) *The Triarchic Mind,* illustrating the use of both Dewey Decimal and Library of Congress (LC) call numbers.

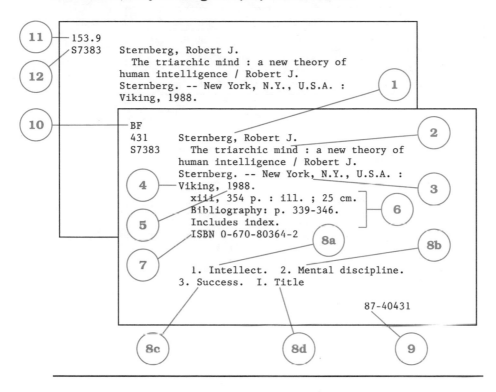

book has been further indexed in the card catalog. The tracings are designed by a cataloging librarian who examines the book, learns what topics it covers, assigns terms known as subject headings to describe the book's contents, and specifies additional access points such as coauthor, editor, or title.

Three *subject headings* have been assigned to Sternberg's book. Indicated by Arabic numbers, they are: Intellect (8a), Mental discipline (8b), and Success (8c). If your library has a divided catalog, these subject headings would be found in the subject catalog. Additionally, there is a tracing for the title of the book (8d) after the Roman numeral "I." Thus, you would find cards in five places in the catalog: listed alphabetically under the author's name, under the book title, and under each of the three subject headings. The entry cards for tracings, as they would appear in most catalogs, are illustrated in Figure 3–B. Note that each card is the same as the author card (the main entry), except that the tracing that provides the index entry location is typed at the top of the card.

The bottom line of the card represented in Figure 3–A contains the Library of Congress card number (9). This is a unique, sequential number assigned to each book processed by the Library of Congress. Each book's LC card number begins with a two-digit code, which typically indicates the year the book was first processed by

FIGURE 3–B

Catalog cards for tracings (i.e., subject headings and title entry), noted in Figure 3–A, for *The Triarchic Mind*.

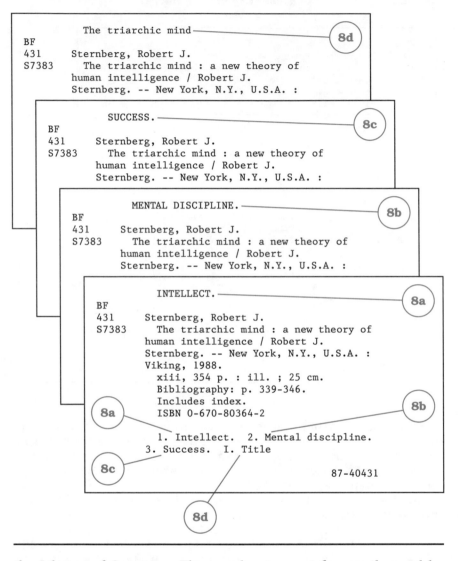

the Library of Congress. The number is most frequently used by librarians in the process of ordering and cataloging books.

The most important piece of information for locating the book in your library is the call number typed in the upper left corner of the card. Libraries using the Library of Congress (LC) classification system type the LC number (**10**) in the upper left corner of each card; libraries using the Dewey Decimal Classification system place the Dewey number (**11**) in the upper corner of each card (see Figure 3–A). In most college libraries, you will be able to go directly to the bookshelves and find the book. In some larger research libraries, however, users are required to place written requests for books that are located and retrieved by a library staff member (a closed-stack system). In most libraries, the call number also reflects the classification system and is indicative of the general subject content of the book.

Classification Systems

The Library of Congress (LC) and Dewey Decimal Classification systems are the most widely used book-classification systems. However, a number of others do exist and are used most frequently in specialized libraries (e.g., medical or agriculture libraries).

The LC classification system uses a combination of letters and numbers. Each entry begins with one or two letters representing a broad class of knowledge, for example, B = Philosophy, BF = Psychology, H = Social Sciences, HM = Sociology, Q = Science, QA = Mathematics, and R = Medicine. These general areas are subdivided by numbers into smaller topics. The Dewey Decimal system uses three-digit numbers ranging from 001 to 999, for example, 100 = Philosophy, 150 = Psychology, 300 = Social Sciences, 370 = Education, and so forth. These areas are subdivided by numbers representing more specific topics. Each LC or Dewey classification number is typically supplemented with one or two Cutter numbers (see Figure 3–A, 12), usually identifying subareas of the subject and finally the author of the book. (In the case of an edited book, in which chapters are written by several persons and collected and edited by one person, the Cutter number is often based on the book's title.) Thus each call number contains two parts: The first is an indication of the book's major topics, and the second is an identifier for the book's author. In many cases, especially if there are different editions of the same book, a date is added and becomes part of the call number. The call number for each book is unique.

The call number for Sternberg's book, based on the LC numbering system, indicates that the book is in the general area of psychology (BF), is in the specific area of intelligence (BF 431), and was written by Robert Sternberg (S7383). We learn essentially the same thing from the Dewey call number.

The Dewey number indicates that the book is in the general area of psychology (150), in the subarea of intellectual and conscious mental processes (153). A particular concern in the book is cognitive processes involving intelligence and aptitude (153.9).

Figure 3–C shows how Sternberg's book would be located by call number in relation to eight other call numbers in the LC system. The call number beginning with B comes before that beginning with BF, and numbers proceed from the smallest to the largest, 40 before 300 before 2000. Cutter numbers are read as though preceded by a decimal point, for example, the following sequence: S246, S44, S463, S7383, S8.

Both the LC and Dewey systems were devised in the late 1800s. Although they have been revised continually, each contains some fundamental curiosities. In the past 100 years, knowledge has grown more in some areas than in others. In 1890, psychology was a new discipline, with its roots in philosophy and in medicine. Thus psychology was classified within the larger groups of philosophy (B in LC, 100 in Dewey) and medicine (R in LC, 610 in Dewey). Also,

FIGURE 3-C

Location by call number of *The Triarchic Mind* in relation to the call numbers of other possible books on the library shelf. (The order proceeds from left to right and top line to bottom line within the call number.)

B	BF	BF	BF	BF	BF	BF	BF	BL
467	87	430	431	431	431	431	637	1
A19	P49	E67	B69	S294	S7383	T273	F82	M277

Sternberg, R. J.
The triarchic mind

materials of possible interest to psychologists may be scattered further about the library, classified with sociology, education, biology, and mathematics. This situation is illustrated in Table 3–B, which presents a sampling of important subareas within psychology and their locations within the LC and Dewey classification systems.

The problem of scatter is compounded by the fact that librarians make judgments in assigning classification numbers and subject headings. Because two persons may make different decisions, books covering several major topics, or in emerging fields, may be assigned different classifications. The fact that both LC and Dewey classification systems undergo periodic revision and change means that not all books will be classified and shelved in the same area over a long period of time. This situation can make your task as a researcher extremely difficult.

Use of Tracings

If you recall that Sternberg's book was indexed under three subject headings—INTELLECT, MENTAL DISCIPLINE, and SUCCESS (see Figures 3–A and 3–B)—you can reasonably assume that other books would also be indexed under the subject headings provided by the tracing. We proceeded in our search by consulting each of these subject headings in the catalog. Figure 3–D illustrates a sampling of three titles found under the subject heading INTELLECT (**8a**). Among these is another view on intelligence, *Frames of Mind* (**13**) by Howard Gardner (**14**), and classified in psychology (BF). We also find a reference book, *Handbook of Intelligence* (**15**), edited by Benjamin B. Wolman (**16**). Under the subject heading MENTAL DISCIPLINE (**8b**), we find a book on sport psychology, *Mental Discipline* (**17**), by Michael K. Livingston (**18**), and classified in Library of Congress class GV. Checking the SUCCESS subject heading (**8c**), we locate two relevant titles: *Self-Fulfilling Prophecies* (**19**) by Russell A. Jones (**20**), and *The Art of Creative Thinking* (**21**) by Robert W. Olson (**22**).

Subject-Headings List

If we had not known of the Sternberg book or another similar starting point, we would have begun the search with the subject catalog. After defining the topic, we would have listed a set of descriptive

TABLE 3-B

Distribution of Psychology-Relevant Materials Throughout the Library in the Library of Congress and Dewey Decimal Classification Systems

Library of Congress Class	Subject Area	Dewey Decimal Class
RC512-571	Abnormal psychology and psychiatric disorders	616.852-616.89
BF636-637	Applied psychology	158
Q334-336	Artificial intelligence	006.3
BF721-723	Child psychology	155.4
BF311	Cognition	153.4
BF660-678	Comparative psychology	156
LB1051-1091	Educational psychology	370.15
TA167	Human factors	620.82
HQ503-1064	Family (social groups)	306.8
HF5548.8	Industrial psychology	158.7
BF501-504	Motivation	153.8
BF1001-1999	Parapsychology and the occult	133
BF231-299	Perception	153.7
BF698	Personality	155.2
HF5549	Personnel management	658.3
QP351-495	Physiological psychology	152
HV689	Psychiatric social work	362.2
RC435-510	Psychotherapy and psychiatry	616.89
BF455-463	Psycholinguistics (psychology of language)	401.9
BF231-299	Sensory perception	152.1
QA278	Statistics (correlation)	519.5
BF39-39.2	psychometrics	150.151
BF237	psychophysics	152.8
RC475-510	Psychotherapy	616.89
HM251-291	Social psychology	302
LC4601-4803	Special education (mentally handicapped and learning disabled children)	371.92
HQ1206-1216	Women, psychology of	155.633

subject terms based on a topic statement (see chapter 2). A primary term with which we might begin would be *intelligence.*

Our next step would be to consult the list of subject headings used in the library. One of the most widely used listings is *Library of Congress Subject Headings,* which is revised annually. This huge, multi-volume set is shelved near the subject catalog in many libraries. (Ask a librarian to point it out if you cannot find it. If your library uses a different system of subject headings, become familiar with that one.) *Library of Congress Subject Headings* is a guide to the *controlled vocabulary* of subject-indexing terms used by the Library of Congress in cataloging books. Only authorized terms contained in the list are used as subject headings and appear as trac-

FIGURE 3–D

Catalog cards of monographs, showing subject headings included in the tracings of *The Triarchic Mind*.

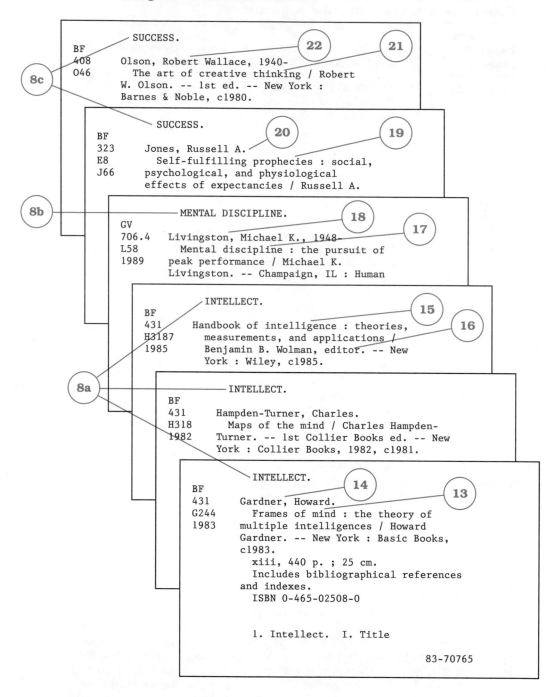

ings on catalog cards. If a descriptive term you wish to use is not included within the controlled vocabulary, then, a synonym may be the authorized term.

To illustrate the use of *Library of Congress Subject Headings,* we begin with the search term *intelligence.* Figure 3–E presents the entry for *Intelligence* (**23**) as it appears in the subject-headings list. The word is in light print with a USE reference (**24**) indicating that this term is not used to index books; instead the entry refers us to the authorized term *Intellect. Intellect* (**25**) is printed in boldface, indicating that it is a main heading. Main headings are used as subject headings to index books in the card catalog. The suggested LC numbers for intelligence in general are BF431 through BF433 (**26**). If your library has an open-stack system, you might browse the shelves in this area to identify relevant materials.

Following the main heading are several types of cross references and subdivisions. The UF (used for) (**27**) tells us that *Human intelligence, Intelligence,* and *Mind* are not used as subject headings. If you had looked up those terms, you would have been referred from those terms to the preferred term, *Intellect.* This cross-reference is consistent with the USE reference (**24**) discussed above. The next cross reference is BT (broader terms) (**28**), meaning that terms such as *Ability* and *Psychology* are broader and more general than *Intellect.* The RT (**29**) list of related terms provides subject headings that are tangential to the subject *Intellect* but still may be relevant to the topic. The SA (see also) (**30**) reference indicates that you may also find relevant books under other subject headings with the subheading *Intelligence levels;* for example, CHILDREN—INTELLIGENCE LEVELS. Under NT (narrower term) (**31**), you will find a list of subject headings with a narrower focus.

The list ends with subdivisions, specific narrow aspects of the main heading. For example, books listed in the card catalog under INTELLECT—GENETIC ASPECTS (**32**) would deal specifically with heredity determinants of intelligence. Cards for books of this type are usually filed alphabetically by subdivision, after all entries under the more general heading INTELLECT. (For further information, consult the introduction in the subject-headings list.)

Other Types of Catalogs

A growing number of libraries no longer rely solely on a catalog of cards. The alternatives include book catalogs, microfiche catalogs, and computerized catalogs. Although these reproduction formats differ from a catalog of index cards, the content of the catalog is typically the same. Each type of catalog provides access to monographs by author, title, and subject and follows the general cataloging rules outlined above.

In the *book catalog,* the index to a library's collections is printed on paper and bound in book form. Frequently, there are separate catalog volumes for each type of entry—author, title, and subject.

Another type of catalog is the *microfiche catalog. Microfiche* is a transparent plastic film sheet, typically 4″ × 6″ in size. Each sheet of microfiche may contain as many as 100 pages of information about thousands of books. A mechanical microfiche reader is needed to enlarge and illuminate the microfiche. If a campus has more than

FIGURE 3–E

Entries from *Library of Congress Subject Headings* (1990), illustrating the identification of terms used as acceptable subject headings in the card catalog.

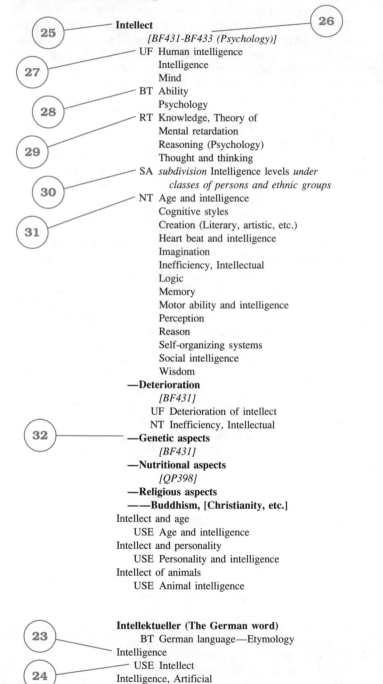

25 **26**

Intellect
  [BF431-BF433 (Psychology)]

27 UF Human intelligence
      Intelligence
      Mind

28 BT Ability
      Psychology

   RT Knowledge, Theory of
      Mental retardation

29   Reasoning (Psychology)
      Thought and thinking

30 SA *subdivision* Intelligence levels *under
         classes of persons and ethnic groups*

   NT Age and intelligence

31   Cognitive styles
      Creation (Literary, artistic, etc.)
      Heart beat and intelligence
      Imagination
      Inefficiency, Intellectual
      Logic
      Memory
      Motor ability and intelligence
      Perception
      Reason
      Self-organizing systems
      Social intelligence
      Wisdom
   —Deterioration
      [BF431]
      UF Deterioration of intellect
      NT Inefficiency, Intellectual
32 **—Genetic aspects**
      [BF431]
   —Nutritional aspects
      [QP398]
   —Religious aspects
   ——Buddhism, [Christianity, etc.]
Intellect and age
   USE Age and intelligence
Intellect and personality
   USE Personality and intelligence
Intellect of animals
   USE Animal intelligence

23 **Intellektueller (The German word)**
      BT German language—Etymology
   Intelligence
      USE Intellect
24 Intelligence, Artificial
      USE Artificial intelligence

one library, a microfiche catalog allows a list of the entire holdings of the library system in each branch library.

The *online computerized catalog* to books is more common in libraries than it was ten years ago. Using a computer terminal and monitor linked to a computer database that contains the bibliographic records of the library's collections, one may search by author, title, subject, editor, and so forth. Due to the expense of converting an entire card catalog to machine-readable form, many libraries rely on a traditional card catalog for older books and an online catalog for more recent titles. Some libraries include certain types of library materials in their automated catalogs (books and journal titles) and not others (government documents). Other libraries have their entire book holdings in their online catalog. When using an online book catalog, consult a reference librarian to determine exactly what is (and what is not) included in the catalog.

Like a card catalog, an online catalog may be searched by author, title, and subject headings. However, an advantage of some online catalogs over their card counterparts is that you may search the library's holdings in many more ways, for example, by International Standard Book Number, publisher, date of publication, or call number. In addition, some catalogs allow you to search for a word or combination of words as they appear in the title or subject headings, without relying solely on a list of acceptable vocabulary such as the *Library of Congress Subject Headings.*

A wide variety of online catalogs is available, and these are often customized to the needs of the individual libraries that utilize them. For that reason, the specifics of searching an online catalog cannot be given here. Many of the strategies used when searching online catalogs are similar to those for preparing a computer search as described in chapter 8, "The Computer Search." Libraries that rely on online catalogs usually produce manuals, brochures, and other aids for their users to help them to use the online catalog effectively.

We have presented the most important basic steps in locating monographs. You should now have enough information to begin searching for books and to do a good job with your search. If you find something that you do not understand, ask a librarian for help.

References

Binet, A., & Simon, T. (1916). *The development of intelligence in children* (E. S. Kite, Trans.). Baltimore, MD: Williams & Wilkins.

Brislin, R. W., Lonner, W. J., & Thorndike, R. M. (1974). *Cross-cultural research methods.* New York: Wiley.

Cattell, R. B. (1971). *Abilities: Their structure, growth, and action.* Boston: Houghton Mifflin.

Guilford, J. P. (1967). *The nature of human intelligence.* New York: McGraw-Hill.

Jensen, A. R. (1969). How much can we boost IQ and scholastic achievement? *Harvard Educational Review, 39,* 1–123.

Kamin, L. J. (1974). *The science and politics of IQ.* Potomac, MD: Erlbaum.

Lewis, M. (1973). Infant intelligence tests: Their use and misuse. *Human Development, 16,* 108–118.

Spearman, C. (1927). *The abilities of man.* New York: Macmillan.

Sternberg, R. J. (1988). *The triarchic mind: A new theory of human intelligence.* New York: Viking.

Terman, L. M. (1916). *The measurement of intelligence.* Boston: Houghton Mifflin.

Thorndike, R. L., & Hagen, E. (1978). *The Cognitive Abilities Test.* Chicago: Riverside.

Thurstone, L. (1938). Primary mental abilities. *Psychometric Monographs* (No. 1). Chicago: University of Chicago Press.

4 *Psychological Abstracts and PsycBOOKS*

Sources Discussed

Thesaurus of psychological index terms (6th ed.). (1991). Washington, DC: American Psychological Association.

Psychological abstracts. (1927–present). Washington, DC: American Psychological Association. Monthly.

Cumulated subject index to Psychological Abstracts, 1927–1960 (2 vols.). (1966). Boston: G. K. Hall.
> *First supplement, 1961–1965.* (1968); *Second supplement, 1966–1968* (2 vols., 1971).

Cumulative subject index to Psychological Abstracts, 1969–1971 (2 vols.). (1972). Washington, DC: American Psychological Association.
> *1972–1974* (2 vols., 1975); *1975–1977* (2 vols., 1978); *1978–1980* (2 vols., 1981); *1981–1983* (3 vols., 1984).

Author index to Psychological Index 1894–1935 and Psychological Abstracts 1927–1958 (5 vols.). (1960). Boston: G. K. Hall.
> *First supplement, 1959–1963* (1965).; *Second supplement, 1964–1968* (2 vols., 1970).

Cumulative author index to Psychological Abstracts, 1969–1971. (1972). Washington, DC: American Psychological Association.
> *1972–1974* (1975); *1975–1977* (1978); *1978–1980* (1981); *1981–1983* (1984).

Psychological index. (1894–1935). Washington, DC: American Psychological Association.

PsycBOOKS. (1987–1990). Washington, DC: American Psychological Association. Annual.

Most published psychological research appears in the form of journal articles. *Psychological Abstracts (PA)* is the most important single index to research in psychology because it provides indexing for specific articles within journals.

PA is published monthly, and it includes monthly as well as cumulated author and subject indexes. For each article indexed, you will find complete bibliographic information and a brief nonevaluative summary of the article.

Although the card catalog is your gateway to books in the library, you cannot find individual chapters within books in the catalog. However, *PsycBOOKS* allows you to locate essays and chapters contained in books by author, title, and subject. Beginning in 1992, book and book chapter coverage will be incorporated into *PA*.

Chapter Example: Eyewitness Testimony

The American criminal justice system places a premium on obtaining the testimony of an eyewitness to a crime. Indeed, eyewitness testimony is often the critical difference between conviction and acquittal. While much testimony is accurate and valuable, mistakes made by eyewitnesses have led to the conviction of innocent people. Loftus (1979) reports numerous cases of conviction in which the testimony of a witness has been of questionable accuracy. What happens to enable an eyewitness to testify? How reliable is that testimony?

The ability to testify about an event relies on memory of an event. How does memory work? A classic representation of memory is as a three-stage process involving acquisition of information, its retention, and subsequent recall. At any step in this process, something may happen that modifies the memory in such a way as to make it an inaccurate reflection of the original event. Additionally, a current conception argues that memory is a constructive process: Information already available in memory colors new information that we add to make it consistent with our conception of the world. As we recall an event, we reconstruct it based on what we think happened (Neisser, 1982).

The first phase of the process is the acquisition of information. An event is witnessed, and information about that event is sensed, perceived, encoded, and stored in memory. However, we cannot attend to everything in a situation. Also, events can occur so rapidly that we are unable to process everything to which we are attending. The possible result is that things that capture our attention in the event are more likely to be those that we store. Factors such as violence involved in an event (Clifford & Scott, 1978) or cultural expectations (Allport & Postman, 1947) can color our perception of an event. Thus, the initial perception of an event may be more or less accurate.

The second phase is retention. For the witness to a crime, the period of time between the event and provision of testimony in a court of law may be months or even years. What happens to memory of the event? Information is added to memory. Some things may be forgotten. Based on a series of experiments in which erroneous information was provided to witnesses, Elizabeth Loftus (Loftus, 1975; Loftus, Miller, & Burns, 1978) argued that new information added during the retention phase can modify the recollection of an event. Thus, it is argued that in the process of repeated questioning by police, attorneys, family, or friends, erroneous information may be provided to the witness which changes his/her recollection of the event.

Retrieval, or recall, is the third phase. Here the witness either describes what he or she can recall of the event or answers questions about what was experienced. In an experimental setting, Loftus and Palmer (1974) demonstrated that the way in which questions were asked would affect a subject's report of what he or she witnessed. Marshall (1966) demonstrated an experimental difference in witness recall attributable to characteristics of the persons asking the questions.

For an eyewitness to testify, the individual must have experienced an event, stored information about that event in memory, retained it for a period of time, and then must recall sufficient information to describe the event or to answer questions about it. Yet many things can happen to an eyewitness that may affect perception and memory of the event and result in testimony that is less than totally accurate.

Others argue that distortions of eyewitness recollection due to the subsequent provision of misleading information are overstated (McCloskey & Zaragoza, 1985; Zaragoza, McCloskey, & Jamis, 1987). In a series of experiments, they found that the provision of misleading information did not have an impact on subjects' ability to recall what they saw. They argue that some of the findings reported by Loftus and others are due to flaws in experimental procedures.

What are the limitations of eyewitness testimony? How reliable are eyewitnesses? What have other researchers reported? This chapter illustrates the use of *Psychological Abstracts (PA)* by focusing on the topic of the reliability of eyewitness testimony.

Thesaurus of Psychological Index Terms: **The Subject Approach**

The first step in a subject search using *PA* is to consult the *Thesaurus of Psychological Index Terms*. Published in 1991, the most recent edition of the *Thesaurus* is the key to the *controlled vocabulary* (words and phrases that have specific meanings and that are authorized for use in subject indexing) of *PA* subject indexes. If a subject-search term you are using is not included in the controlled vocabulary, then that term will not be used to index materials in *PA*, and you will not find any citations, even though relevant research may have been published. Therefore, you must ascertain which of your subject-search terms will be useful.

The *Thesaurus* contains three major parts: the Relationship Section, the Rotated Alphabetical Terms Section, and the Alphabetical Term Clusters Section. Begin by examining the Relationship Section, where terms are listed alphabetically. The term most closely associated with our topic is *eyewitnesses*. Figure 4–A presents an excerpt from the *Thesaurus* containing the entry for *Eyewitnesses*. The term is in light print with the note, "Use Witnesses" (**1**). This cross-reference directs you from an unused term to one that is a subject heading used in *PA*. We then turn to the entry for *Witnesses* in the Relationship Section, which is in boldface type (**2**). Underneath the term, the *scope note* (SN) provides an exact definition of the term as it will be used in the controlled vocabulary for *PA* subject indexing (**3**). The entry also tells us the term is used for (UF) the concept *Eyewitnesses* (**1a**), which is consistent with our earlier attempt to find that term. *Thesaurus* entries also can assist you in locating related terms (R), in this case, *Legal Evidence* and *Legal Testimony* (**4**). Under some subject headings are also listed broader (B), more general terms (**5**) or narrower (N), more specific terms (**6**) that are related to the concept, although these do not appear under *Witnesses*. Often, terms listed as narrower or related terms are pre-

FIGURE 4–A

***Thesaurus of Psychological Index Terms* (6th ed., 1991, pp. 81, 237), Relationship Section, illustrating subject-indexing terms contained in the controlled vocabulary and showing notes and cross-references.**

RELATIONSHIP SECTION

Eyeblink Reflex [73]
PN 252   **SC** 18940
  UF Blink Reflex
  B   Reflexes [71]
  R   Startle Reflex [67]

Eyelid Conditioning [73]
PN 404   **SC** 18950
SN Conditioned eye blinking or the classical conditioning paradigm resulting in conditioned eye blinking.
  UF Conditioning (Eyelid)
  B   Classical Conditioning [67]   ⑤

Eyewitnesses   ①
  Use Witnesses

• • •

Withdrawal (Defense Mechanism) [73]
PN 95   **SC** 56860
SN Psychoanalytic term describing the escape from or avoidance of emotionally or psychologically painful situations.
  B   Defense Mechanisms [67]   ⑧

Within Subjects Design   ② ⑨
  Use Repeated Measures

Witnesses [85]   ③
PN 271   **SC** 56885
SN Persons giving evidence in a court of law or observing traumatic events in a nonlegal context. Also used for analog studies of eyewitness identification performance, perception of witness credibility, and other studies of witness characteristics having legal implications.   ⑩
  UF Eyewitnesses   ①ᵃ
  R | ↓ Legal Evidence [91]   ④
    | ↓ Legal Testimony [82]   ⑦

Wives [73]
PN 1286   **SC** 56900
  B   Family Members [73]
      Human Females [73]
      Spouses [73]   ⑥
  N   Housewives [73]

ceded by down arrows (↓) (**7**). By looking in the Relationship Section under these terms, you will find narrower, more specific subject headings.

The number 85 (**8**) following *Witnesses* indicates that the term was added to the controlled vocabulary in 1985. Thus, when you search subject indexes published before 1985, you must use search terms other than *witnesses*. The *postings note* (PN) (**9**) indicates the number of times that this term has been assigned to citations in *Psychological Abstracts* and its machine-readable counterparts from the first time it was used in 1985 through June 1990. This is potentially very useful information: A frequently used descriptor may be too broad and may cover many irrelevant references, whereas an infrequently used descriptor may yield too few relevant references. Finally, each *Thesaurus* term used as a descriptor is assigned a unique, five-digit *subject code* (SC) (**10**), which can be used when searching the machine-readable equivalent of *PA* (*PsycINFO*).

The second part of the *Thesaurus*, the Rotated Alphabetical Terms Section, is especially helpful for identifying the correct entry for concepts expressed by several words or a phrase. In this section, illustrated in Figure 4–B, each significant word in a multiple-word indexing phrase appears in its proper alphabetical order. Entries in the subject indexes, however, are alphabetically arranged only by the first word in each indexing phrase. All terms that are part of the *Thesaurus* controlled vocabulary (**2a**) and those that are not (**1b**) are represented in this section. Terms that are not used are in italics and accompanied by a star, indicating that you need to consult the Relationship Section for the proper term. In the case of multiword subject headings or phrases, such as *Legal Testimony*, the phrase will appear more than once; in this case, under *legal* (**4a**) and under *testimony* (**4b**).

The Alphabetical Term Clusters Section lists most *Thesaurus* terms under eight broad categories: *Disorders, Educational, Geo-*

FIGURE 4–B
Entries from the *Thesaurus of Psychological Index Terms* (6th ed., 1991, pp. 266, 278, 309, 314), Rotated Alphabetical Terms Section, showing the correct entry form for multiple-word terms.

ROTATED ALPHABETICAL TERMS SECTION

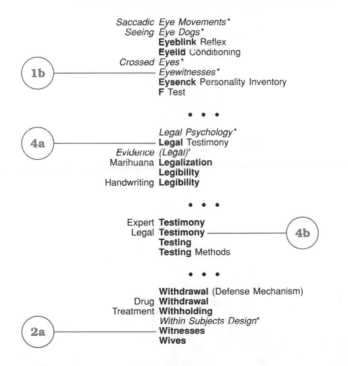

graphic, *Legal, Occupational and Employment, Statistical, Tests and Testing, and Treatment.* These are in turn subdivided into a total of 61 subclusters. For example, the *Legal* cluster contains eight subclusters, as illustrated in Figure 4–C (**11**). One of the these is *Adjudication* (**12**), under which you will find the subject heading, *Witnesses* (**2b**). The purpose of the Clusters Section is to group similar terms under broad concepts, allowing you to scan them quickly and begin with a few relevant indexing terms. Because the Clusters Section functions as a sort of index to subject heading terms, it is still necessary to check the terms you find in the Relationship Section of the *Thesaurus.* In addition, only about 60% of the *Thesaurus* subject headings terms are represented in the Clusters Section.

Having selected our terms from the *Thesaurus,* we can begin a subject search in a monthly issue of *PA,* looking for information indexed under the subject term, *Witnesses.*

Using *Psychological Abstracts*

The table of contents in the monthly issues of *PA* indicates that articles in *PA* are arranged under broad subject categories, for example, *Physical and Psychological Disorders.* This particular category is further divided into narrower subcategories, for example, *Mental Disorders* and *Speech and Language Disorders.* To find citations on a more specific concept, however, we will have to consult the Brief Subject Index, located in the back of the monthly issue.

FIGURE 4–C

Selected entries from the Legal Cluster of the Alphabetical Term Clusters Section in the *Thesaurus of Psychological Index Terms* (6th ed., 1991, p. 324).

CLUSTERS SECTION

LEGAL CLUSTER

(**11**)
- Adjudication
- Criminal Groups
- Criminal Offenses
- Criminal Rehabilitation
- Laws
- Legal Issues
- Legal Personnel
- Legal Processes

(**12**) **Adjudication**

Adjudication
Capital Punishment
Commitment (Psychiatric)
Competency to Stand Trial
Crime Victims
Criminal Conviction
Criminal Justice
Criminal Responsibility
Defendants

• • •

Legal Detention
Legal Evidence
Legal Processes
Legal Testimony
Parole
Polygraphs
Probation
(**2b**) Witnesses

As shown in Figure 4–D, the term *Witnesses* (**2c**) is listed in the Brief Subject Index of the December 1989 issue. Following the term are 10 numbers, known as entry numbers, corresponding to sources indexed in this issue of *PA*. To illustrate how to use this index, we start by finding entry number 38908 (**13**), although in an actual search we would eventually check all 10 entry numbers. In each issue of *PA*, citations are listed consecutively by the entry number, which appears at the beginning of the citation. Each entry consists of two major parts: the bibliographic information, which will enable us to locate the publication, and a nonevaluative *abstract* summarizing the article.

Following the entry number (**13a**) in Figure 4–D are the authors' names (**14**), arranged with last name first and, in parentheses, the affiliation of the first author at the time the article was written and

FIGURE 4–D

Subject- and author-index listings and an article entry from *Psychological Abstracts* (Vol. 76, December 1989, pp. xxxi, xxxix, xli, 3728).

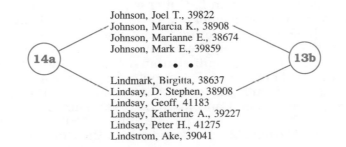

BRIEF SUBJECT INDEX   (13)

(2c) ——— **Witnesses** 38908, 39558, 39806, 39807, 39808, 39809, 39816, 39823, 39825, 39829
Wives 38661, 39766, 39776

HUMAN EXPERIMENTAL PSYCHOLOGY   (14)

(13a) ——— 38908. **Lindsay, D. Stephen & Johnson, Marcia K.** (Williams Coll, Bronfman Science Ctr, Williamstown, MA) **The eyewitness suggestibility effect and memory for source.** *Memory & Cognition,* 1989(May), Vol 17(3), 349–358. —In 2 experiments, 253 undergraduates who served as misled or control Ss were tested either with a yes/no recognition test or with a "source monitoring" test designed to orient Ss to attend to information about the sources of their memories. Results demonstrate that suggestibility effects obtained with a recognition test can be eliminated by orienting Ss toward thinking about the sources of their memories while taking the test. Although misled Ss were capable of identifying the source of their memories of misleading suggestions, they nonetheless sometimes misidentified them as memories derived from the original event.

(15) (16) (17) (20) (18) (19)

AUTHOR INDEX

Johnson, Joel T., 39822
Johnson, Marcia K., 38908
Johnson, Marianne E., 38674
Johnson, Mark E., 39859

• • •

Lindmark, Birgitta, 38637
Lindsay, D. Stephen, 38908
Lindsay, Geoff, 41183
Lindsay, Katherine A., 39227
Lindsay, Peter H., 41275
Lindstrom, Ake, 39041

(14a)   (13b)

submitted for publication (**15**). In this example the first author, D. Stephen Lindsay, was affiliated with the Bronfman Science Center at Williams College. The title of the article, "The eyewitness suggestibility effect and memory for source" (**16**), is followed by information about the article's publication. This article by Lindsay and Johnson was published in the journal *Memory and Cognition* (**17**), in May 1989 (**18**), Volume 17, issue number 3 (**19**), on pages 349 through 358 (**20**). Each entry for a journal article in *PA* employs this bibliographic format. Following the citation is a brief abstract of the article.

Volume Indexes to *Psychological Abstracts*

When a volume of *PA* is completed (when all 12 issues have been published for the year), cumulated volume indexes are compiled. A check of the term *Witnesses* (**2d**) in the annual cumulated subject index to Volume 75 (January–December 1988) is illustrated in Figure 4–E. Note that the volume-cumulated Subject Index provides more information about each entry than the monthly Brief Subject Index. Each article is represented by a phrase containing basic information about the article: for example, independent and dependent variables, the subject population studied, article format, and other terms and phrases important in the study. The last listing under the subject heading *Witnesses* represents a study on "prelineup interview or lineup context cues reinstatement procedures & encoding & storage & retrieval variables," their effect on "eyewitness identification accuracy," using a study population "college students" (**21**). This entry, number 7324 (**22**), appears to be relevant to our search.

Entries are numbered sequentially throughout the issues of each volume, beginning with entry 1 in issue 1. As illustrated in Figure 4–E, entry 7324 (**22a**) is listed under the general subject category of "Social Processes and Social Issues" (**23**). This article has three authors: Brian L. Cutler (**24**), Steven D. Penrod (**25**), and Todd K. Martens (**26**), whose institutional affiliation is Florida International University at North Miami (**27**). As in the preceding example, the citation continues with the title of the article (**16a**), the name of the journal in which the article appears (**17a**), the year and month of publication (**18a**), the volume and issue numbers (**19a**), and the page numbers (**20a**). Following this information is the abstract. In this case, the abstract is reprinted from the journal in which the complete text of the article was published (**28**).

Author Indexes to *Psychological Abstracts*

If we had known that Brian L. Cutler or any of his associates had written on eyewitness memory, we could have used the Author Index to Volume 75. In the Author Index, the author and co-author of each article included in the volume are listed in alphabetical order by surname. Several entries from the Author Index to Volume 75 are illustrated in Figure 4–E. The entry for the first author, Brian L. Cutler, provides full bibliographic information for the article he co-authored with Penrod and Martens (**24a**), entry number 7324 (**22b**). The Author Index also contains abbreviated entries for Penrod (**23a**) and Martens (**26a**), referring us to the Cutler entry 7324

FIGURE 4-E

Annual subject- and author-index listings from *Psychological Abstracts* (Vol. 75, January–December 1988, pp. 2258–2259, pp. 240, 649, 775) and an article entry from March 1988 (Vol. 75, no. 3).

VOLUME 75

Widowers   SUBJECT INDEX   Witnesses

(2d) — **Witnesses**

age & ability to distinguish fact from fantasy & memory, competency to testify, child witnesses, implications for role of child psychiatrists, 4234

• • •

(21)
order of individual & dyadic collaborative recall of police interrogation scene & individual confidence vs validity, testimonial validity of dyadic effort, college students, England, 10649

prelineup interview or lineup context cues reinstatement procedures & encoding & storage & retrieval variables, eyewitness identification accuracy, college students, 7324 ——————— (22)

(23) — *SOCIAL PROCESSES AND SOCIAL ISSUES*   (25)

(24)   (26)

(22a)
7324. **Cutler, Brian L.; Penrod, Steven D. & Martens, Todd K.** (Florida International U, North Miami) **Improving the reliability of eyewitness identification: Putting context into context.**   (16a)

(27)
Journal of Applied Psychology, 1987(Nov), Vol 72(4), 629–637.
—We examined the effects of context reinstatement procedures on eyewitness identification accuracy. Subjects were 290 undergraduates who viewed a videotaped reenactment of a liquor store robbery and, in a later session, attempted to identify the robber from a lineup parade. Two types of context reinstatement procedures were examined together with eight encoding, storage, and retrieval variables manipulated within the stimulus videotape and the lineup procedures. Disguise of the robber impaired identification accuracy ($p < .05$). There was a significant interaction between disguise and the context reinstatement interview ($p < .01$) such that the context reinstatement interview had a stronger impact on identification accuracy in the high-disguise condition. Lineup cues interacted with lineup composition ($p < .05$), retention interval ($p = .01$), and exposure to mug shots ($p = .05$; although in a manner contrary to our expectation). These interactions indicated that lineup context cues improved identification accuracy in the high-similarity, 2-week retention interval, and no mug-shots conditions.—*Journal abstract.* ——— (28)

(17a)   (20a)   (19a)   (18a)

VOLUME 75
AUTHOR INDEX

(24a) — **Cutler, Brian L.;** *Penrod, Steven D. & Martens, Todd K.* Improving the reliability of eyewitness identification: Putting context into context. *Journal of Applied Psychology, 1987(Nov), Vol 72(4), 629–637.*   7324 ——— (22b)

• • •

(26a) — **Martens, Rainer**—*See* Burton, Damon 1157
Martens, Todd K.—*See* Cutler, Brian L. 7324 ——— (22c)

• • •

(25a) — **Penrod, Steven D.**—*See* Cutler, Brian L. 7324, 19956, 26399
Penson, Jennifer—*See* Spear, Linda P. 3882

(22c). To verify that this article was relevant to our topic, we would locate the complete entry with abstract, as found earlier by using the Subject Index.

Similarly, as illustrated in Figure 4–D, we would have used the Author Index in recent issues of *PA* to locate articles by D. Stephen Lindsay or Marcia K. Johnson (14a). Such a search would have yielded entry 38908 (13b) in Volume 76, December 1989, the same article we identified when we used the Brief Subject Index.

The author indexes to *PA* are especially helpful for locating studies by individuals who are well known in a particular area of research. As noted in the Chapter Example section earlier, Elizabeth Loftus, among other researchers, has contributed a considerable body of literature in the area of eyewitness testimony. Using the author indexes, we can locate many of her journal article publications. The author indexes are also helpful when locating articles for which you have incomplete bibliographic information; for example, you may have the author's name, the article title, and name of the journal, but not the year, volume, or pages in which it was published. When using this approach, however, keep in mind that articles may be listed in a *PA* issue many months after the article's original publication. This is due to backlogs in processing, journal publication and mailing delays, or other problems. Therefore, you may have to consult several volumes of *PA* to find the information you need.

Extending the List of Search Terms

If we had attempted to search in a *PA* pre-1985 Subject Index using the term *witnesses,* we would have found nothing because this indexing term was introduced into the *PA* controlled vocabulary in 1985. How could we search for our topic in pre-1985 *PA*? We would have to consult other, less specific terms included in the pre-1985 controlled vocabulary. Unfortunately, we could expect that, although useful, they would produce many irrelevant entries. What could we use as these subject-search terms? Looking back at the *Thesaurus* entry for *Witnesses* in Figure 4–A, a related term was *Legal Testimony* (4). Although this term is less precise, it still is relevant to our search topic.

The *PA* volume covering 1983 is illustrated in Figure 4–F. There are several entries under the subject heading *Legal Testimony* (4a) that concern eyewitness testimony. One in particular looks interesting because it concerns eyewitness accuracy and will discuss the impact and implications of psychological research (29). The article is also a literature review, meaning that the author(s) focus on presentation and discussion of relevant research literature. This reference carries the entry number 12587 (30). This item in *PA* Volume 70 (30a) refers us to an article by Gary L. Wells (31) and Donna M. Murray (32) at the University of Alberta (33). It contains the standard bibliographic information, including article title (16b), journal name (17b), year and issue month (18b), volume and issue number (19b), and pages (20b). Until recently, the number of references appended to articles was noted at the end of the *PA* abstract (34). Although many irrelevant citations are included under the more

FIGURE 4-F

An early article on eyewitness testimony cited in *Psychological Abstracts* (Vol. 70, December 1983, p. 497) and its subject- and author-index listings (*Psychological Abstracts Index*, Vol. 70, July–December 1983, pp. 43, 65, 497–498).

SUBJECT INDEX

(4a) — **Legal Testimony** [See Also Expert Testimony]

    ability to estimate credibility of eyewitness testimony, prospective jurors, 3322

    accuracy of eyewitness testimony, child vs adult traffic accident witnesses, literature review, 10198

    classification of verbal response modes during direct & cross-examination, attorneys & rape victims, 10189

    competence as trial witness & reliability of evidence, mentally handicapped 22 yr old female, 5903

(29) — criticism of Neil v Biggers criteria for judging eyewitness accuracy & relevant psychological research, literature review, 12587 — **(30)**

    demand characteristics created by misleading questioning, accuracy of eyewitness testimony, college students, 7991

    information introduced after event, eyewitness testimony, college students, 3323

    knowledge of empirical evidence vs common sense in eyewitness testimony, lawyers vs jurors, 5573

    problems with use of hypnosis, murder suspect, 1029

    psychological factors, eyewitness identification, 12570

    use of hypnosis in legal testimony, 5579

---

(31)   **(32)**

SOCIAL PROCESSES AND SOCIAL ISSUES

  (33)

(30a) — 12587. **Wells, Gary L. & Murray, Donna M.** (U Alberta, Edmonton, Canada) **What can psychology say about the *Neil v. Biggers* criteria for judging eyewitness accuracy?** *Journal of Applied Psychology,* 1983(Aug), Vol 68(3), 347–362.—In an influential case (*Neil vs Biggers*, 1972), the US Supreme Court identified 5 criteria to be considered in judging eyewitness identification evidence: the witness's certainty, degree of attention, opportunity to view the assailant, the accuracy of prior description, and the amount of time elapsed between an event and identification. Although the Court's intuitions about eyewitness identification are not unreasonable, the recent growth of a literature using forensically relevant procedures has increased the gap between experimental evidence and the *Biggers* criteria.

(34) — (82 ref)

(16b) **(17b)** **(18b)** **(20b)** **(19b)**

AUTHOR INDEX

    Murphy-Berman, Virginia, 6006

    Murray, David M., 5448

(32a) — Murray, Donna M., 12587

    Murray, Edward J., 10699

    Wellman, Mary M., 3204

    Wells, Carl F., 1815

    Wells, G. B., 10543

(31a) — Wells, Gary L., 12587

    Wells, Gordon, 790

general search term, *Legal Testimony*, we can use it to continue searching successfully in other pre-1985 *PA* subject indexes.

As the excerpt in Figure 4–F indicates, the author indexes in older *PA* cumulated volumes differ from recent volume author indexes. In the case of Volume 70 for 1983, the entries for both Wells (**31a**) and Murray (**32a**) contain only entry numbers.

Cumulated Indexes to *Psychological Abstracts*

By now you have probably gathered that this process is going to be laborious and time-consuming, and you may wonder whether any shortcuts exist. At the beginning of the chapter, we listed a number of cumulated or cumulative indexes. The cumulated subject and author indexes can be very useful for retrospective searching. Instead of checking numerous volume indexes, you can check the less numerous cumulated indexes. The cumulated subject indexes have the same organization as the volume indexes and use the same subject headings; however, each entry includes the *PA* volume and entry number. Thus, had we checked the *Cumulative Subject Index to Psychological Abstracts, 1981–1983*, we would have found the same entry by Wells and Murray under the subject heading *Legal Testimony* that was noted in Figure 4–F. Here the entry would be listed as 70:12587, indicating that the information is contained in *PA*, Volume 70, and has the entry number 12587.

The cumulated author indexes are useful for building a retrospective bibliography of publications by a specific author. Figure 4–G presents several sample entries for Elizabeth F. Loftus as they appear in the 1981–1983 cumulative. During this indexing period, Loftus published several relevant articles on eyewitness testimony and on the accuracy of memory in relating events.

FIGURE 4–G

Entries for E. F. Loftus from the *Cumulated Author Index to Psychological Abstracts, 1981–1983* (p. 453).

Loftus, Elizabeth F. & *Burns, Terrence E.* Mental shock can produce retrograde amnesia. *Memory & Cognition, 1982(Jul), Vol 10(4), 318–323.*   69:9653

Loftus, Elizabeth F.; *Greene, Edith & Smith, Kirk H.* How deep is the meaning of life? *Bulletin of the Psychonomic Society, 1980(Apr), Vol 15(4), 282–284.*   65:9612

Loftus, Elizabeth F. & *Greene, Edith.* Warning: Even memory for faces may be contagious. *Law & Human Behavior, 1980, Vol 4(4), 323–334.*   66:11952

35

Loftus, Elizabeth F. Impact of expert psychological testimony on the unreliability of eyewitness identification. *Journal of Applied Psychology, 1980(Feb), Vol 65(1), 9–15.*   65:5336

Loftus, Elizabeth F. & *Marburger, Wesley.* Since the eruption of Mt. St. Helens, has anyone beaten you up? Improving the accuracy of retrospective reports with landmark events. *Memory & Cognition, 1983(Mar), Vol 11(2), 114–120.*   70:11888

Loftus, Elizabeth F. Memory and its distortions. *G. Stanley Hall Lecture Series, 1982, Vol 2, 119–154.*   70:7193

Loftus, Elizabeth F. Natural and unnatural cognition. *Cognition, 1981(Aug–Dec), Vol 10(1–3), 193–196.*   67:11310

Loftus, Elizabeth F. Reactions to blatantly contradictory information. *Memory & Cognition, 1979(Sep), Vol 7(5), 368–374.*   65:420

Loftus, Elizabeth F. The malleability of human memory. *American Scientist, 1979(May–Jun), Vol 67(3), 312–320.*   65:467

Loftus, Elizabeth F.—*See* Cole, William G. 65:2658
Loftus, Elizabeth F.—*See* Deffenbacher, Kenneth A. 68:10267
Loftus, Elizabeth F.—*See* Greene, Edith 68:7287
Loftus, Elizabeth F.—*See* Hilgard, Ernest R. 65:2697

As we have noticed, publications are often written by two or more co-authors. Some of the relevant articles listed in Figure 4–G were co-authored by Loftus and one or two other authors (**35**). It is possible that these individuals have written other relevant articles. In addition, there are several cross-references at the bottom of this list to items that were co-authored by Loftus but of which she was not the primary author (**36**). We can thus expand our author search by including co-authors when checking *PA* indexes.

The cumulated index contains the complete bibliographic information for each entry. If you wish to check the abstract to determine whether the article is relevant, the index provides the *PA* volume and entry numbers. You will find this information important if your library does not own a particular journal and you must judge whether to request an article through interlibrary loan (see chapter 11).

Subject Scope of *Psychological Abstracts*

Since it was initiated in 1927, *PA* has become the most comprehensive indexing tool available to access the published literature of psychology. Selected sources from related disciplines, such as biology, education, management, medicine, psychiatry, social work, and sociology, are also included in *PA*. Each month *PA* staff members scan hundreds of journals and documents in these related fields. When they determine that a particular article or document relates to psychology, they include it in *PA*. Table 4–A includes examples of materials from two categories: relevant (Psychology) and related (Fringe) (APA, 1987).

Examining Table 4–A, we note that smoking behavior is a topic that could logically be pursued in *PA* because it concerns human behavior. You would find useful information on the related topic of nicotine pharmacology in *PA*; for example, its effects on reaction time and affect in humans. However, you might also need to consult a more appropriate indexing tool in another discipline. (For more information about related sources, see Chapter 5.)

Background on *Psychological Abstracts*

The coverage that *PA* provides of the professional literature of psychology is continually expanding. The increase in the number of items represented in *Psychological Abstracts* may be readily seen in

TABLE 4–A

Topics Included in *Psychological Abstracts* as Relevant or Related to Psychology

Relevant	Related
Sexual behavior	Sexual hormones
Smoking behavior	Nicotine pharmacology
Visual discrimination	Eye disorders
Verbal communication	Linguistics
Man–machine systems	Technology and work

Note: The *PsycINFO Users Manual* (1987, p. 1-1) uses the terms *Psychology* and *Fringe*, respectively.

FIGURE 4–H

Number of entries included in *Psychological Abstracts* in seven different years, showing the increase in coverage of *Psychological Abstracts* and reflecting an increase in publications. (Note: Unlike 1970, 1980 does not include dissertations and books and 1989 does not include foreign-language articles.)

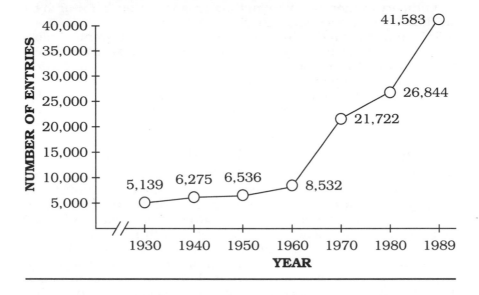

Figure 4–H, which notes the number of entries appearing in 1 year of *PA* at 10-year intervals since 1930. Since 1960, publishing in psychology has had an especially rapid growth.

The 1969–1971 *Cumulative Subject Index* noted that, during that 3-year period, over 800 journals and 1,200 books, dissertations, and other materials were scanned for possible inclusion. In 1981, approximately 1,000 journals were regularly scanned. By 1988, that number had increased to over 1,400 titles representing more than 25 languages.

The increasing volume of research material and corresponding increases in costs of producing the monthly *PA* issues and cumulated indexes have dictated some recent changes in coverage. Before 1980, *PA* incorporated citations to books, chapters within books, and citations to doctoral dissertations. These were represented in the subject and author indexes and (in the case of book volumes) abstracted just like references to journal articles. Although books and dissertations are important to the literature of psychology, these formats were no longer included in the print *PA* after 1980. Books and book chapters published 1987 through 1990 are indexed in *PsycBOOKS*, which is described later in this chapter.

Doctoral dissertations, which are typically not published, are an important part of the original research literature of psychology. Until 1980, *PA* provided access to dissertations relevant to psychology in *Dissertation Abstracts International (DAI)*. Therefore, it is likely that you will encounter citations to *DAI* in any retrospective literature search you undertake in *PA*. Figure 4–I shows some typical citations for doctoral dissertations (**37**), one of which is on wit-

FIGURE 4–I
Entries for doctoral dissertations and a foreign-language publication from *Psychological Abstracts* (Vol. 60, August 1978, pp. 260, 263).

EXPERIMENTAL PSYCHOLOGY (HUMAN)

Learning & Memory

2362. **Cornell, John E.** (U Southern Mississippi) **Individual differences and control processes in human recognition memory.** *Dissertation Abstracts International,* 1977(Mar), Vol 37(9-B), 4722.

• • •

(40) ——— 2364. **Denis, Michel.** (CNRS, Lab de Psychologie de la Culture, Paris, France) **[The operation of teen-aged ——— (41) representation as a source of interference in memorizing significant simple data.]** (Fren) *Psychologie Française,* 1976, Vol 21(1–2), 83–97. —Investigated the differential memory of 168 university students for picture and word stimuli. Mnemonic activity improved when an image corresponded to its verbal description. —*K. J. Hartman.* (42)

(37) ——— 2365. **Doggett, David E.** (U Virginia) **The interaction of successive retrievals from semantic memory.** *Dissertation Abstracts International,* 1977(Apr), Vol 37(10-B), 5394–5395.

• • •

(38) ——— 2388. **Peterson, Mark A.** (U California, Los Angeles) **Witnesses: Memory of social events.** *Dissertation Abstracts International,* 1977(Jun), Vol 37(12-B, Pt 1), 6409. ——— (39)

ness memory (**38**). These citations refer us to the appropriate citation in *DAI* (**39**), where you will find a lengthy abstract describing the research. Entries for doctoral dissertations, however, are still included in the machine-readable equivalent of *PA*, the PsycINFO database. These citations are retrievable by a computer search. (for details, see chapter 8). You may also rely on the printed *DAI* index to locate citations to doctoral dissertations, lengthy abstracts, and ordering information (see chapter 10).

Another major change in coverage occurred with the 1988 volume. As noted above, journals representing research published in over 25 languages are indexed and abstracted. However, the increasing volume of foreign-language publishing, the lag time involved in providing English-language abstracts for all entries, and their corresponding tardy appearance in *PA* led to the decision to discontinue their inclusion in the print source. You will encounter them in older volumes of *PA*. Figure 4–I contains an example of a French-language article by Michel Denis (**40**). The translated title is placed in brackets (**41**) and the original language of publication is noted in parentheses (**42**). (After September 1982, the article title in the original language was included in addition to the translated title). Like dissertations, foreign-language citations are included in the machine-readable *PsycINFO* database. They are also part of the *PsycLIT* database (see chapter 8).

Finally, we have noted that the primary format covered in *PA* is the journal article. In addition to articles, research reports or monographs that are part of series are also included. Two examples are the *Monographs of the Society for Research in Child Development* and the *Research Monographs Series* of the National Institute on Drug Abuse. Technically speaking, these are not journals. However, they are published on a regular schedule and contain subject-relevant articles. Articles within annual review volumes are also included (see chapter 2 for discussion of annual reviews).

The researcher whose topic requires a historical overview of the research may be interested in the predecessor to *PA*. *Psychological Index*, originally published in connection with the scholarly journal *Psychological Review*, began in 1894 as an annual bibliography of psychology and related topics. It was a bibliographic supplement to the *Review*, published by the American Psychological Association, and it continued to appear after *PA* was initiated in 1927. *Psychological Index* ceased publication after its 1935 volume was issued because of a decision by the APA that the two sources were duplicative. After 1935, access to psychological literature was provided by *PA*.

Searching for Book Chapters: *PsycBOOKS*

As we noted in chapter 3, research appearing in journal articles has certain advantages to that published in book form. Books often take longer to organize, write, and publish than journal articles, so that the lag time between the research conducted and the publication of results is significantly longer. Although the card catalog provides access to books, books may contain chapters contributed by several different individuals who write on various aspects of a topic. Papers and lectures presented at professional and research conferences and symposia are frequently collected and published in the form of a book. As much as 30% of the published information in psychology is produced in the form of books and book chapters (APA, 1990). When *Psychological Abstracts* discontinued coverage of books after 1980, it became difficult to obtain information on books and book chapters in psychology.

The purpose of *PsycBOOKS* is to index and provide abstracts and tables of contents for books published in a given year. The first annual edition of *PsycBOOKS* was published in 1989 and included over 1,423 books published in 1988. (A retrospective volume covering books published in 1987 was produced in 1989.) Annual editions covering books from the previous year were also published in 1990 and 1991.

There are two types of entries: those representing entire book volumes and those for chapters within books. Each year of *Psyc-BOOKS* consists of five volumes, four of these devoted to broad areas of psychology: *Experimental Psychology: Basic and Applied; Developmental, Personality, and Social Psychology; Professional Psychology: Disorders and Treatment;* and *Educational Psychology and Health Psychology*. The fifth volume consists of the indexes: subject, author, book title, and publisher. The first four volumes list entries under topical subdivisions, and each of these is represented

FIGURE 4–J
Subject and author index listings and a book chapter entry on eyewitness memory in *PsycBOOKS* (1989, pp. III-445, V-49, V-353).

1989
SUBJECT INDEX

(43) **Witnesses**

Analysis of the statements of victims,
   witnesses and suspects.   III 7100-63
The cognitive interview technique for
   victims and witnesses of crime.   III 7100-149
Criteria-based statement analysis.   III 7100-152

(44) Field studies of eyewitness memory of
   actual crimes.   III 7100-162 (45)
Hazards in detecting deceit.   III 7100-163
Investigative hypnosis.   III 7100-168
Legal issues in eyewitness evidence.   III 7100-170

---

(46) ***FORENSIC PSYCHOLOGY & LEGAL ISSUES***   **7100-158 – 7100-165** (56)
7100

(45a) **162. Field studies of eyewitness memory of actual crimes.** (44a)
Cutshall, Judith & Yuille, John C. [In: (7100-138) Psychological (49)
methods in criminal investigation and evidence. *Raskin, David
C. (Ed.)* Springer Publishing Co, Inc: New York, NY, USA, (50)
(47) 1989. xvi, 399 pp. ISBN 0-8261-6450-1 (hardcover).] pp. 97-
124.
[from the introduction] (51)
(48) — presents a series of studies of eyewitness performance
  and memory in criminal cases that brings together
(52)   knowledge from laboratory studies of witness behavior (54)
  and data gathered from police and psychologist interviews of witnesses to actual crimes
[from the chapter] (55)
(53) — focus on eyewitness memory research and its applicabil-
  ity to real-life situations ◇ briefly consider the current
  status of eyewitness research, its ecological validity, and
  the implications of generalizing research findings to actual witness situations

---

1989
AUTHOR INDEX

Cutler, Anne, I, 5300-92; I, 5400-18
Cutler, Neal E., II, 6200-526
 Cutshall, Judith, III, 7100-63; III,
  7100-162
Cutter, Mary Ann Gardell, IV, 7600-
  129
Cytrynbaum, Solomon, I, 5900-196

• • •

Yufit, Robert I., III, 6800-674
Yuh, William, III, 6800-244
 Yuille, John C., III, 6700-2; III,
  7100-63; III, 7100-162
Yuki, Gary, I, 5900-139
Yule, William, IV, 7300-414

by a broad classification number. For example, the volume covering professional issues contains sections for *Clinical Psychological Testing,* classification code 6700, and *Mental & Psychological Disorders,* classification code 6800. Obviously, these categories are too broad to allow browsing for relevant material. Therefore, use of the Subject Index in Volume V is essential to find items specific to your topic. Fortunately, the Subject Index uses the same controlled vocabulary as *PA;* that is, the *Thesaurus of Psychological Index Terms.*

Turning to the subject index in Volume V of *PsycBOOKS 1989,* we notice that there are several titles listed under the term *Witnesses* (**43**) in Figure 4–J. One in particular concerns eyewitness memory: "Field studies of eyewitness memory of actual crimes" (**44**). This is entry number III 7100-162 (**45**), indicating that the reference is in Volume III, entry 7100-162. We turn to Volume III, classification code section 7100, which represents *Forensic Psychology & Legal Issues* (**46**). References are thereunder listed by entry number. Within entry 162 (**45a**), we find the title of the chapter (**44a**), which is by Judith Cutshall (**47**) and John C. Yuille (**48**). This is a chapter in a book titled *Psychological Methods in Criminal Investigation and Evidence* (**49**) edited by David C. Raskin (**50**). The entry also notes that the book was published by Springer Publishing Company in New York in 1989 (**51**) and has 16 prefatory pages and 399 pages of text (**52**). The ISBN for the hardbound edition is provided (**53**). The chapter by Cutshall and Yuille is on pages 97 through 124 (**54**). In addition to bibliographic information, the entry contains brief excerpts from the book's introduction and from the chapter itself (**55**) that describe this chapter's scope and content. Figure 4–J also illustrates the Author Index for the 1989 *PsycBOOKS,* in which we find that entry III 7100-162 is among the entries for Judith Cutshall (**47a**) and for John C. Yuille (**48a**).

Entry 7100-162 contains a cross-reference to the *PsycBOOKS* entry for the edited book in which this chapter is included. The bibliographic information indicates that the chapter appeared in entry 7100-138 (**56**). Because we may be interested in other chapters in this volume, we turn to this entry (**56a**), which is illustrated in Figure 4–K. In addition to the bibliographic information already noted, we find out considerably more about the book, including the institutional affiliation of the editor, David C. Raskin (**57**). There is also a brief description of the book's contents (**58**).

This entry also reproduces the book's table of contents, including the titles and authors of other chapters. One of these, the chapter by Cutshall and Yuille, we have already located as *PsycBOOKS* entry number 7100-162 (**45b**). The chapter titled "The Psychology of Eyewitness Testimony," by Elizabeth F. Loftus, Edith L. Greene, and James M. Doyle (**59**), is also relevant to our topic. To find out more about this chapter, we would look in *PsycBOOKS 1989* for entry 7100-178 (**60**).

The Author Index provides access to individuals who are editors as well as authors. In this case, this book, entry 7100-138 (**56b**), is among the entries under David C. Raskin (**57a**). *PsycBOOKS 1989* provides an index by book title, including the book edited by Raskin (**49a**), entry 7100-138 (**56c**).

After the 1990 set was published in 1991, APA decided to discontinue *PsycBOOKS* and incorporate its coverage into existing

FIGURE 4–K
Author- and book-title-index listings and a book entry, including table of contents with contributors, on forensic psychology, in *Psyc-BOOKS* (1989, pp. III-441,V-36, V-372). (Note reference to entry 7100-162 illustrated in Figure 4–J.)

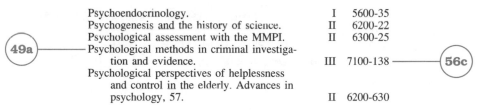

1989
AUTHOR INDEX

57a

Rapoport, Tamar, II, 6200-458
Rapp, Dorrie, IV, 7700-313
Raskin, David C., III, 7100-37; III,
7100-138; III, 7100-174
56b Raskin, Nathaniel J., III, 6900-562
Raslear, Thomas G., I, 5500-67

1989
BOOK TITLE INDEX

49a

Psychoendocrinology.	I	5600-35
Psychogenesis and the history of science.	II	6200-22
Psychological assessment with the MMPI.	II	6300-25
Psychological methods in criminal investigation and evidence.	III	7100-138 ——— **56c**
Psychological perspectives of helplessness and control in the elderly. Advances in psychology, 57.	II	6200-630

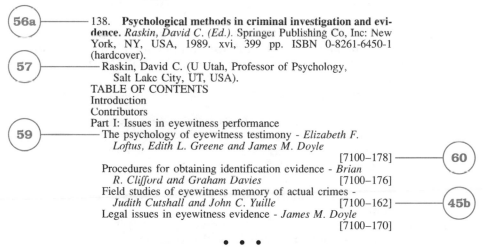

FORENSIC PSYCHOLOGY & LEGAL ISSUES   7100-137 – 7100-140
7100

56a —— 138. **Psychological methods in criminal investigation and evidence.** *Raskin, David C. (Ed.).* Springer Publishing Co, Inc: New York, NY, USA, 1989. xvi, 399 pp. ISBN 0-8261-6450-1 (hardcover).

57 —— Raskin, David C. (U Utah, Professor of Psychology, Salt Lake City, UT, USA).
TABLE OF CONTENTS
Introduction
Contributors
Part I: Issues in eyewitness performance

59 —— The psychology of eyewitness testimony - *Elizabeth F. Loftus, Edith L. Greene and James M. Doyle*
[7100–178] ——— **60**
Procedures for obtaining identification evidence - *Brian R. Clifford and Graham Davies*   [7100–176]
Field studies of eyewitness memory of actual crimes - *Judith Cutshall and John C. Yuille*   [7100–162] ——— **45b**
Legal issues in eyewitness evidence - *James M. Doyle*
[7100–170]

• • •

Index
58 *[from the introduction]* This book provides the scientific and professional communities with current psychological knowledge, and the current legal status, of major methods used for investigation and evidence in law enforcement and other legal situations, many of which are complex and controversial. It includes in-depth summaries and analyses of the scientific literature on topics such as eyewitness perception and memory, identification procedures, interview techniques, and credibility

• • •

sources. Beginning with the January 1992 issue, citations to books and book chapters will again be included in *Psychological Abstracts*. The format of book and chapter citations and abstracts will resemble the *PsycBOOKS* format, rather than the *PA* format for journal articles. The entire 4-year run of *PsycBOOKS* will also be added to *PsycLIT* on CD-ROM in 1992, and future *PsycLIT* updates will include book and chapter coverage.

The chapters that follow describe sources that supplement *PA* and *PsycBOOKS*. These contain useful information in areas of psychology that overlap with other fields such as education, management, medicine, and sociology. Additional specialized sources are included in Appendix A.

References

Allport, G. W., & Postman, L. J. (1947). *The psychology of rumor.* New York: Henry Holt & Co.

American Psychological Association. (1987). *PsycINFO user manual.* Washington, DC: Author.

American Psychological Association. (1990). *PsycBOOKS 1989.* Washington, DC: Author.

Clifford, B. R., & Scott, J. (1978). Individual and situational factors in eyewitness testimony. *Journal of Applied Psychology, 63,* 352–359.

Loftus, E. F. (1975). Leading questions and the eyewitness report. *Cognitive Psychology, 7,* 560–572.

Loftus, E. F. (1979). *Eyewitness testimony.* Cambridge, MA: Harvard University Press.

Loftus, E. G., Miller, D. G., & Burns, H. J. (1978). Semantic integration of verbal information into visual memory. *Journal of Experimental Psychology: Human Learning and Memory, 4,* 19–31.

Loftus, E. F., & Palmer, J. C. (1974). Reconstruction of automobile destruction: An example of the interaction between language and memory. *Journal of Verbal Learning and Verbal Behavior, 13,* 585–589.

Marshall, J. (1966). *Law and psychology in conflict.* New York: Bobbs-Merrill.

McCloskey, M., & Zaragoza, M. (1985). Misleading postevent information and memory for events: Arguments and evidence against memory impairment hypotheses. *Journal of Experimental Psychology: General, 114,* 1–16.

Neisser, U. (1982). Memory: What are the important questions? In U. Neisser (Ed.), *Memory observed* (pp. 3–19). San Francisco: W. H. Freeman.

Zaragoza, M., McCloskey, M., & Jamis, M. (1987). Misleading postevent information and recall of the original event: Further evidence against the memory impairment hypothesis. *Journal of Experimental Psychology: Learning, Memory and Cognition, 13,* 36–44.

5 Psychology-Related Indexing and Abstracting Tools

Many problems that psychologists study are complex and multifaceted. Some lend themselves to investigation by many individual disciplines as well as to interdisciplinary inquiry. While some questions are specific to psychology, related questions may be posed from a slightly different point of view by researchers in fields such as education, sociology, business, and the health sciences. As researchers report results of studies to colleagues in their own professions, bodies of literature are built on related aspects of a topic through the journals and conferences of related fields.

Certain areas of psychology regularly intersect with other disciplines. For example, research in education may be relevant to the educational psychologist and management literature to the industrial–organizational psychologist or consumer psychologist. Abnormal and social psychologists may need to examine literature in sociology, while physiological, clinical and comparative psychologists may find literature in the health sciences relevant. The psychological researcher who does not consult this related literature may overlook important findings.

Although *Psychological Abstracts (PA)* is the primary index to psychological literature, indexing and abstracting services in related areas are of potential interest to psychologists. This chapter illustrates the use of several sources in fields related to psychology. It is divided into four sections, presenting sources that provide access to literature in education, management, health sciences, and sociology. We begin by focusing on the general topic of stress. We selected stress because it is one example of a problem which has been investigated by researchers in many fields who have taken many different approaches. As we discuss each related field, a particular aspect of stress will be used to illustrate a search in that field.

Education, & Welfare, 1967, p.184). Today, 16 ERIC clearing-houses, each responsible for a particular subject area, cover a broad range of interests and many types of research produced in a variety of formats, whether or not sponsored by the government. Many psychologists are interested in ERIC's coverage of educational psychology, testing, counseling, child development, and evaluation research.

ERIC provides three important services for the researcher. The first is *Resources in Education (RIE,* formerly *Research in Education),* published monthly with annual cumulated indexes. *RIE* indexes and abstracts conference proceedings, position papers, research reports, curriculum guides, books, doctoral dissertations, and other types of materials collected and indexed by ERIC clearinghouses.

The second service is *document delivery.* More than 800 libraries (primarily college and university libraries) in the United States, Canada, and abroad subscribe to the ERIC Document Microfiche Collection, which makes available most documents indexed in *RIE.* On a monthly basis, subscribing libraries receive shipments of microfiche for documents included in recent issues of *RIE.* Subscribing libraries are listed in the *Directory of ERIC Information Service Providers.* Copies of most ERIC documents, available in paper copy or microfiche, are also sold by the ERIC Document Reproduction Service at a reasonable cost.

The third ERIC service is *Current Index to Journals in Education (CIJE).* First published in 1969, *CIJE* provides access to over 750 journals in education and related disciplines. Subject and author indexes in *CIJE* and *RIE* appear in each monthly issue and are cumulated.

Thesaurus of ERIC Descriptors

The source of controlled vocabulary for both *RIE* and *CIJE* is the *Thesaurus of ERIC Descriptors.* We begin our search by consulting this volume. Using the search term *test anxiety,* we examine the Alphabetical Descriptor Display section of the *Thesaurus,* which is an alphabetical list of the controlled vocabulary, *descriptors,* in ERIC's subject indexes. We find this term in boldface capital letters (**1**) in Figure 5–A, indicating that it is an acceptable subject heading. The term has been part of the ERIC controlled vocabulary since March 1980 (**2**). Since that time, it has been used to index 238 documents in *CIJE* (**3**) and 171 documents in *RIE* (**4**). As with the *Thesaurus of Psychological Index Terms,* you can use this information to determine if the headings you select are too broad (with the possibility of many irrelevant references) or too narrow (not enough citations relevant to the topic). The scope note (SN) (**5**) provides a brief explanation of the term's index usage. Broader terms are listed under BT (**6**), and related terms (RT) follow (**7**). Some entries also include narrower terms (NT) (**8**). The UF ("used for") (**9a**) and USE (**9**) cross references, although not included under the heading TEST ANXIETY, are illustrated in nearby entries.

To supplement the terms listed below the descriptor, we could also consult the Descriptor Group Code (GC) section of the *Thesaurus* (**10**). These codes represent broad concepts under which related

FIGURE 5-A

Entries from the *Thesaurus of ERIC Descriptors* (12th ed., 1990, pp. 267–268, 300–301, 474).

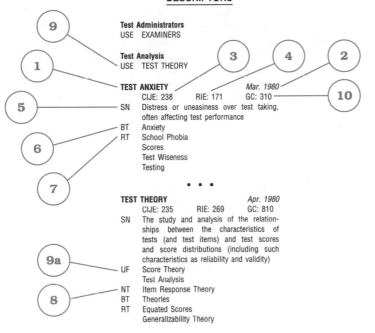

DESCRIPTORS

Test Administrators
USE   EXAMINERS

Test Analysis
USE   TEST THEORY

TEST ANXIETY   *Mar. 1980*
        CIJE: 238   RIE: 171   GC: 310
SN   Distress or uneasiness over test taking,
        often affecting test performance
BT   Anxiety
RT   School Phobia
        Scores
        Test Wiseness
        Testing

• • •

TEST THEORY   *Apr. 1980*
        CIJE: 235   RIE: 269   GC: 810
SN   The study and analysis of the relation-
        ships between the characteristics of
        tests (and test items) and test scores
        and score distributions (including such
        characteristics as reliability and validity)
UF   Score Theory
        Test Analysis
NT   Item Response Theory
BT   Theories
RT   Equated Scores
        Generalizability Theory

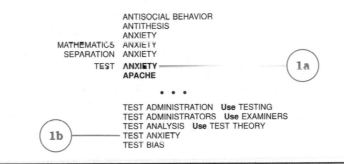

ROTATED DISPLAY OF DESCRIPTORS

                        ANTISOCIAL BEHAVIOR
                        ANTITHESIS
                        ANXIETY
MATHEMATICS   ANXIETY
    SEPARATION   ANXIETY
            TEST   **ANXIETY**
                        APACHE

• • •

TEST ADMINISTRATION   **Use** TESTING
TEST ADMINISTRATORS   **Use** EXAMINERS
TEST ANALYSIS   **Use** TEST THEORY
TEST ANXIETY
TEST BIAS

descriptors are listed. We would use the GC primarily with a computer search to expand the list of search terms. (For further information, consult the ERIC *Thesaurus.*)

Another useful feature in the *Thesaurus* is the Rotated Descriptor Display (similar to the Rotated Alphabetical Terms section of the *Thesaurus of Psychological Index Terms;* see chapter 4). It is especially helpful for identifying multiword terms that describe your topic, whether or not they are part of the ERIC controlled vocabulary. The example in Figure 5–A contains two sections from the Rotated Display of Descriptors, both referring to our *test anxiety* term. One section lists terms preceding our keyword *anxiety* (**1a**), and another lists keywords following *test* (**1b**). Although this section of the *Thesaurus* will refer you from an unacceptable to an acceptable term by using the USE cross reference, it is advisable to check the USE term in the Alphabetical Descriptor Display for the scope note and lists of broader, related, and narrower terms.

Some items indexed in the ERIC publications are assigned identifiers in addition to *Thesaurus* descriptors. *Identifiers* are words or phrases that help describe the content of a document or article but for which no adequate descriptor exists. They may be proper names (such as the name of a specific test), personal names, geographic areas, or terminology so new that a *Thesaurus* descriptor has not yet been coined. Some of these identifers will appear in the subject indexes to *RIE* and *CIJE* and therefore will have document numbers listed for them. Because identifiers are not standardized and not consistently assigned to documents in the same way as descriptors, your best approach is to limit your search terms to *Thesaurus* terms first.

Having found relevant, acceptable indexing terms by using the *Thesaurus,* we can now use these terms for searching *RIE* and *CIJE* subject indexes.

Resources in Education (RIE)

Presented in Figure 5–B is a portion of the *RIE* Subject Index (Vol. 23). It shows several document title entries, listed in alphabetical order, that follow the heading *Test Anxiety* (**1c**). Among these entries is "Exam Performance as a Function of Exam Completion Time . . ." (**11**), which appears to be relevant to our search. This entry, like each ERIC document, is assigned a unique accession number, beginning with the letters ED (ERIC Document) and followed by a six-digit number (**12**). The accession number refers us to the appropriate entry in the Document Resume section.

Document resumes, listed sequentially by *ED accession number,* provide bibliographic information and a lengthy abstract for each document. Figure 5–C presents the *RIE document resume* for the title that interests us, ED 189 478. The ERIC accession number (**12a**) is at the upper left-hand corner of the entry. An additional number (**13**), assigned by the ERIC clearinghouse that originally processed the document, appears at the upper right-hand corner. This is a temporary accession number given before an ED number

FIGURE 5–B

Subject index entries from *Resources in Education Annual Cumulation 1988: Index* (1989, p. 495).

SUBJECT INDEX

(**1c**) — **Test Anxiety**
　Communicative Talk in Interview-Type Assessment of
　　Spoken English.　　　　　　　　　　ED 296 576
　A Descriptive Study of Community College Students Coping with Examination Stress.　　　　　　ED 291 039
　The Effectiveness of Stress Management and Test-Taking
　　Workshops in Reducing Test Anxiety of Community
　　College Students.　　　　　　　　　ED 292 819
(**11**) — Exam Performance as a Function of Exam Completion　(**12**)
　　Time, State Anxiety and Ability.　　　ED 290 117

FIGURE 5-C

Portions of a document resume from *Resources in Education* (Vol. 23, June 1988, p. 28.)

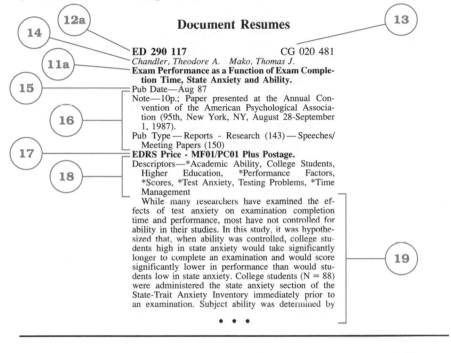

Document Resumes

ED 290 117   CG 020 481

Chandler, Theodore A.   Mako, Thomas J.

Exam Performance as a Function of Exam Completion Time, State Anxiety and Ability.

Pub Date—Aug 87

Note—10p.; Paper presented at the Annual Convention of the American Psychological Association (95th, New York, NY, August 28-September 1, 1987).

Pub Type — Reports - Research (143) — Speeches/ Meeting Papers (150)

EDRS Price - MF01/PC01 Plus Postage.

Descriptors—*Academic Ability, College Students, Higher Education, *Performance Factors, *Scores, *Test Anxiety, Testing Problems, *Time Management

    While many researchers have examined the effects of test anxiety on examination completion time and performance, most have not controlled for ability in their studies. In this study, it was hypothesized that, when ability was controlled, college students high in state anxiety would take significantly longer to complete an examination and would score significantly lower in performance than would students low in state anxiety. College students (N = 88) were administered the state anxiety section of the State-Trait Anxiety Inventory immediately prior to an examination. Subject ability was determined by

• • •

has been assigned. Such clearinghouse numbers occasionally appear in a document abstract referring to related documents in a series. Bibliographic information, including the name(s) of the author(s) (**14**), the title (**11a**), and the publication date (**15**), follows. The Note and Pub Type (**16**) describe the source and the type of the document. EDRS Price (**17**) indicates that this item is available for purchase from the ERIC Document Reproduction Service. MF01/ PC01 are price codes needed for ordering this document. You should check the price list in the most recent issue of *RIE* for current prices. In some cases, entries will include the organization where the document originated, the agency sponsoring its preparation, alternate sources for obtaining the document, and other information.

Subject terms assigned to this document are listed as Descriptors (**18**). A maximum of six major descriptors, indicated by asterisks (*), may be assigned to a document and used as subject headings in print indexes. Finally, a lengthy abstract (**19**) summarizes the document's contents.

We can use the list of major descriptors in the document resume to modify our list of subject-search terms. This list is especially helpful because, if you recall, the term "Test Anxiety" was not used until March 1980 (see Figure 5-A) and expanding a search to cover material before this date will require the use of other terms.

Many libraries own ERIC documents on microfiche. These are arranged according to the six-digit ED number. If your library does not own a collection of ERIC microfiche, a reference librarian may refer you to a library that does.

FIGURE 5-D

Subject Index entries from the *Current Index to Journals in Education* (Vol. 22, issue 5, May 1990, p. 231).

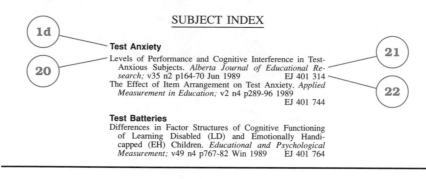

SUBJECT INDEX

Test Anxiety
Levels of Performance and Cognitive Interference in Test-Anxious Subjects. *Alberta Journal of Educational Research;* v35 n2 p164-70 Jun 1989   EJ 401 314
The Effect of Item Arrangement on Test Anxiety. *Applied Measurement in Education;* v2 n4 p289-96 1989
                                                EJ 401 744

Test Batteries
Differences in Factor Structures of Cognitive Functioning of Learning Disabled (LD) and Emotionally Handicapped (EH) Children. *Educational and Psychological Measurement;* v49 n4 p767-82 Win 1989   EJ 401 764

Current Index to Journals in Education

The *Current Index to Journals in Education (CIJE)*, similar in approach to *RIE*, indexes journal literature. Figure 5–D shows two entries from the Subject Index of the May 1990 issue of *CIJE*, listed under the descriptor *Test Anxiety* (**1d**). The article "Levels of Performance and Cognitive Interference in Test-Anxious Subjects" (**20**) appears to be relevant to our topic. However, limited information for each article is provided by this index (**21**); for example, the name of the author is missing. Therefore, we use the *CIJE* accession number (**22**) to locate more complete information in the Main Entry Section of *CIJE*, where entries are listed sequentially by their ERIC Journal (EJ) accession numbers.

Figure 5–E illustrates this article as it appears in the Main Entry Section of the May 1990 issue. The EJ number (**22a**) appears at the beginning of the entry. The number on the right side is the ERIC clearinghouse number (**12a**). This number is followed by the title of the article (**20a**), the name of the author (**23**), and the full citation (**21**). Also provided is a list of descriptors assigned to this article (**24**). Three identifiers were also assigned to this article (**25**), repre-

FIGURE 5-E

A citation from the Main Entry section of *Current Index to Journals in Education* (Vol. 22, issue 5, May 1990, p. 81).

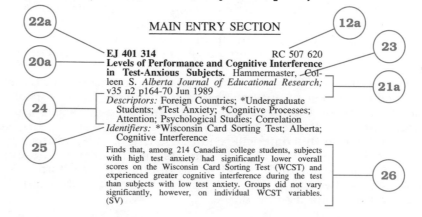

MAIN ENTRY SECTION

EJ 401 314   RC 507 620
Levels of Performance and Cognitive Interference in Test-Anxious Subjects. Hammermaster, Colleen S. *Alberta Journal of Educational Research;* v35 n2 p164-70 Jun 1989
Descriptors: Foreign Countries; *Undergraduate Students; *Test Anxiety; *Cognitive Processes; Attention; Psychological Studies; Correlation
Identifiers: *Wisconsin Card Sorting Test; Alberta; Cognitive Interference

Finds that, among 214 Canadian college students, subjects with high test anxiety had significantly lower overall scores on the Wisconsin Card Sorting Test (WCST) and experienced greater cognitive interference during the test than subjects with low test anxiety. Groups did not vary significantly, however, on individual WCST variables. (SV)

senting the name of the testing instrument used, the geographic origin of the study, and a concept not represented by a *Thesaurus* descriptor. A brief summary of the article's content (26) helps us to evaluate the relevance of this source to our search.

Another Approach to *RIE* and *CIJE*

Suppose that you are able to begin a search with a relevant source. Rather than start with the *Thesaurus,* you could first locate the document in *RIE* or *CIJE* by using the author or institution indexes in *RIE* or the author or journal contents indexes in *CIJE.* (For some years, an *RIE* title index may be available.) Then you could review the list of major descriptors assigned to your source in the Main Entry or Document Resume sections to create or modify a list of relevant subject-search terms. As a double check, you could consult the *Thesaurus* for other potentially relevant terms and proceed with the search.

Education Index

Some libraries subscribe to *Education Index (EI),* published by H. W. Wilson, as an alternative to *CIJE.* Initiated in 1929, published monthly and cumulated annually, *EI* is especially useful for searching education journal literature published before 1969. Some students find *EI* easier to use than *CIJE,* possibly because of its similarity to the *Readers' Guide to Periodical Literature.* There is no thesaurus. Author and subject entries are included in the same alphabetical index with "see" cross references directing the user from unused terms to authorized subject headings. In 1975, a section indexing book reviews was added to the back of each issue and bound volume. *EI* has its limitations, however. It covers only the core journals in education and special education (about 300 titles) and, therefore, has a much more limited scope than *CIJE.* Furthermore, it provides no abstracts.

FIGURE 5–F

Entries from *Education Index* (Vol. 38, July 1987–June 1988 cumulation, pp. 1346, 1349, 1357).

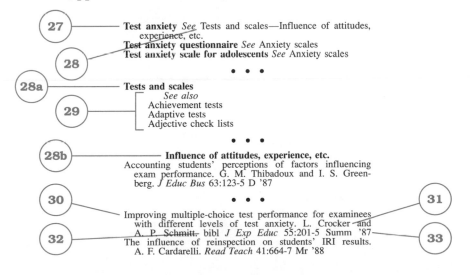

We begin searching *EI* by looking under the term *Test anxiety* (**27**). Instead of references, we find a "see" reference (**28**), directing us to the acceptable subject heading, "Tests and scales—Influence of attitudes, experience, etc." as illustrated in Figure 5–F. *Tests and scales* is printed in boldface type, indicating that it is an acceptable subject heading (**28a**). Several "See also" references (**29**) refer us to alternate, more specific subject headings, if these are more appropriate. Citations are arranged alphabetically by title under the subtopic, "Influence of attitudes, experience, etc." (**28b**). A reference potentially relevant to our topic is "Improving multiple-choice test performance for examinees with different levels of text anxiety" (**30**), written by L. Crocker and A. P. Schmitt (**31**). The citation shows that the article contains a bibliography (**32**). The remaining information (**33**), including journal name, volume number, pages on which the article appears, and date of publication, completes the article reference. A list of abbreviations used in *EI* appears in the front of each issue, as well as a list of abbreviations of publications indexed. Because journal titles are often abbreviated in *EI* citations, you should consult the list so that you will not try to locate a journal that does not exist.

Management

Source Discussed

Business periodicals index. (1958–present). New York: H. W. Wilson. Monthly (except August), cumulated annually.

Section Example: Managerial Stress

Managers, especially lower- and middle-level managers, are subjected to numerous stressors on a regular basis. They experience significant pressures from both their supervisors and subordinates. They are often eager to succeed and feel responsible for the successes of their subordinates. Frequently, however, they have little control over organizational demands or resources which contribute to or inhibit the successes of their work group. They may experience stress as a function of work overload, long hours, travel, organizational or role conflict, or responsibility for people. Many managers are exposed to stress so routinely that they are unaware of it and its consequences (Albrecht, 1979; Ivancevich & Matteson, 1980).

Managerial stress leads to a variety of negative consequences in organizations. Stress-induced cognitive distortions such as over-generalization, personalization, reduced creativity, and impaired judgment and decision making may lead to reduced organizational effectiveness and lost opportunities (Beech, 1987; Ivancevich & Matteson, 1980; Janis, 1982; Mandler, 1982).

Ivancevich, Matteson, Freedman, and Phillips (1990) reviewed a variety of workplace stress-management interventions and provided a framework for understanding types of workplace stress in relation to interventions. Stress-management intervention techniques in organizations include relaxation training, meditation, biofeedback, exercise, work redesign, time management, goal setting, and organizational change (e.g., Albrecht, 1979; Cooper, 1987; Ivancevich et al., 1990).

FIGURE 5–G

Entries from *Business Periodicals Index* (Vol. 32, issue 5, January 1990, p. 666).

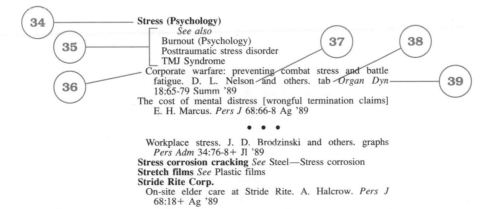

In this section, we focus on literature addressing coping strategies for managers dealing with workplace stress.

Business Periodicals Index

Business Periodicals Index (BPI) provides access to more than 300 publications of three types: trade and industry journals; research journals in business, management, accounting, finance, and related areas; and selected journals from related disciplines. Monthly and annually cumulated issues provide alphabetical indexing by subject. The organization of *BPI* is similar to *Education Index* and other indexes published by H. W. Wilson.

Using the January 1990 issue of *BPI* as an example, the subject heading *Stress (Psychology)* (**34**) contains three "See also" cross references (**35**) to related subjects, as illustrated in Figure 5–G. These are followed by several relevant citations listed in alphabetical order by title. One citation that may deal with our topic is "Corporate warfare: Preventing combat stress and battle fatigue" (**36**), written by D. L. Nelson and others (**37**). The citation indicates that the article contains a table (**38**). The entry also includes the abbreviated journal title, the volume number, the page numbers, and the publication date (**39**). You can decipher the abbreviations by consulting a list in the front of each issue and volume of *BPI*.

Medicine

Sources Discussed

Index medicus. (1960–present). Bethesda, MD: U.S. National Library of Medicine. Monthly.

Cumulated index medicus. (1960–present). Bethesda, MD: U.S. National Library of Medicine. Annual.

Abridged index medicus. (1970–present). Bethesda, MD: U. S. National Library of Medicine. Monthly.

Cumulated abridged index medicus. (1970–present). Bethesda, MD: U. S. National Library of Medicine. Annual.

Medical subject headings. (1960–present). Bethesda, MD: U.S. National Library of Medicine. Annual.

List of journals indexed in Index Medicus. (1960–present). Bethesda, MD: U.S. National Library of Medicine. Annual.

Section Example: Stress as a Factor in Coronary Heart Disease

Stress has been implicated as a risk factor in a variety of health problems, one of which is coronary heart disease. Heart attack is a significant cause of death in the United States, and stress has been suggested as a contributing factor, given its role in causing changes in heart rate, blood pressure, and serum cholesterol (Greenberg, 1983). The link between stress and fluctuations in catecholamines and norepinephrine suggests a stress role in coronary heart disease (Holroyd & Lazarus, 1982; Rosenman & Chesney, 1982). A significant relationship has also been reported among Type A behavior, stress, and coronary heart disease (Rosenman & Chesney, 1982).

Levi (1987) argues, however, that although "acute stress can precipitate angina pectoris, arrhythmias, congestive heart failure, stroke, myocardial infarction, or sudden cardiac death in those who already have cardiovascular disease" (pp. 84–85), the specific role of chronic stress in coronary heart disease itself is not well documented. Additionally, the relationship between stress and genetic predisposition to coronary heart disease is not well understood (Farber, 1982). Stress has, however, been identified as only one of a number of risk factors related to coronary heart disease. Others include high blood pressure, high cholesterol level, cigarette smoking, being overweight, and family history of heart disease (Veninga & Spradley, 1981).

In this section, we will focus on the role of prolonged stress as a causal factor in coronary heart disease, and the relationship between stress and other risk factors such as smoking and alcohol consumption in coronary heart disease.

Index Medicus

Index Medicus provides coverage of approximately 3,000 biomedical journals worldwide. Monthly issues are cumulated annually in *Cumulated Index Medicus.* For smaller libraries, *Abridged Index*

FIGURE 5-H
Subject headings from *Medical Subject Headings* (*MeSH*) (1990, p. 493).

(40) ——— **STRESS**
C23.280.853+
GENERAL ADAPTATION SYNDROME was see under STRESS &
ADAPTATION, PHYSIOLOGICAL 1963–74
XU GENERAL ADAPTATION SYNDROME

STRESS DISORDERS, POST-TRAUMATIC
F3.709.438.180.680+
81; was NEUROSES, POST-TRAUMATIC 1963–80; COMBAT
DISORDERS was heading NEUROSES, WAR 1963–80
X NEUROSES, POST-TRAUMATIC
X POST-TRAUMATIC STRESS DISORDERS
X PTSD
XU COMBAT DISORDERS

STRESS FRACTURES see FRACTURES, STRESS

• • •

(41)

STRESS PROTEINS see HEAT-SHOCK PROTEINS

(42) **STRESS, PSYCHOLOGICAL**
F2.830.900+   F3.126.903+
73; was STRESS, PSYCHOLOGIC 1969–72

(43) ——— see related
CROWDING
LIFE CHANGE EVENTS
X EMOTIONAL STRESS

(44)

STRESSFUL EVENTS see LIFE CHANGE EVENTS

Medicus includes articles from more than 100 English-language journals and is cumulated annually as *Cumulated Abridged Index Medicus.*

We begin our search by consulting *Medical Subject Headings (MeSH)* to verify that our search terms correspond to subject headings, which are illustrated in Figure 5–H. Acceptable subject headings are printed in large boldface type, whereas unacceptable terms appear in small type. Figure 5–H lists several subject headings, the most general of which is STRESS (**40**). A more specific term, and one that more closely matches our topic, is STRESS, PSYCHOLOGICAL (**41**). This subject heading has been used since 1973 and was preceded by use of another term (**42**). The entry also refers us to two related *MeSH* subject headings (**43**) and tells us that this heading is used for the concept EMOTIONAL STRESS (**44**). For explanations of other notations, see the "Introduction" to *MeSH.*

Each month, *Index Medicus* is published in two parts: a listing of references by subject and another by author. The multivolume *Cumulated Index Medicus (CIM)* contains separate volumes for subject and author listings. Searching the 1989 *CIM* under our subject heading (**41a**), as illustrated in Figure 5–I, we find that most references are listed under subheadings, one of which is COMPLICATIONS (**45**). A relevant article is "Diet, tobacco, alcohol, and stress as causes of coronary artery heart disease" (**46**) by W. D. Lynch and others (**47**). The entry provides complete bibliographic information including the abbreviated journal title, the date of publication, the volume and issue number (in parentheses), and journal page num-

FIGURE 5–I

Citations from the Subject Index of *Cumulated Index Medicus* (Vol. 30, Book 10, 1989, pp. 12308–12310).

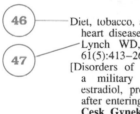

1989   CUMULATED INDEX MEDICUS   STRESS, PSYCHOLOGICAL

STRESS, PSYCHOLOGICAL (41a)

   see related
      CROWDING
      LIFE CHANGE EVENTS
   Self-report and stability of physical symptoms by adolescents. Marschall P. **Adolescence** 1989 Spring; 24(93):209–16
   Mechanisms of physical and emotional stress. Based on the proceedings of an NIH symposium. November 6–8, 1986, Bethesda, Maryland. **Adv Exp Med Biol** 1988;245:1–530

• • •

COMPLICATIONS (45)

   Acute chest pain without obvious organic cause before the age of 40. Respiratory and circulatory response to mental stress. Roll M, et al. **Acta Med Scand** 1988;224(3):237–43
   The role of life events in the myasthenia gravis outcome: a one year longitudinal study. Magni G, et al. **Acta Neurol Scand** 1989 Apr;79(4):288–91
   Rapidly developing overweight in school children as an indicator of psychosocial stress. Mellbin T, et al. **Acta Paediatr Scand** 1989 Jul;78(4):568–75

• • •

(46) Diet, tobacco, alcohol, and stress as causes of coronary artery heart disease: an ecological trend analysis of national data.
(47) Lynch WD, et al. **Yale J Biol Med** 1988 Sep–Oct; (48) 61(5):413–26
[Disorders of the menstrual cycle in women after entering a military training center. III. FSH, LH, prolactin, estradiol, progesterone and psychological stress 2 months (49) after entering the center] Čížková J, et al. **Cesk Gynekol** 1988 Sep;53(8):556–60 (Eng. Abstr.) **(Cze)**

bers (48). *Index Medicus* provides extensive coverage of foreign-language journals. Citations to these articles follow all others under subject headings and subheadings, and their translated titles are surrounded by brackets (49). Journal titles are frequently abbreviated. For complete titles, you should consult *List of Periodicals Indexed in Index Medicus*, which is also reprinted annually in the first volume of *CIM*.

Sociology

Sources Discussed

Sociologial abstracts. (1953–present). San Diego, CA: Sociological Abstracts. Five issues per year, annually cumulated indexes.

Thesaurus of sociological indexing terms (2nd ed.). (1989). San Diego, CA: Sociological Abstracts.

Section Example: Stress in Divorce

The concept of family is changing. The divorce rate has increased considerably since 1950 (U.S. Bureau of the Census, 1990), and many families experiencing divorce include children (Greenberg, 1983). Divorce is a significant element in the Social Readjustment Rating Scale (Holmes & Rahe, 1967). Divorce can result from a variety of stressors, for example, the work stress on family life. The process of divorce itself may induce stress in family members. Despite work by Croog (1970) and by Wallerstein and Kelley (1980) on divorce-related stress, much remains to be learned. This chapter focuses on the impact of divorce as a stressor on families.

Sociological Abstracts

Sociological Abstracts (SA) is the primary index for literature in sociology and its related disciplines. It includes articles in 1,200 serial publications (e.g., scholarly journals, annual reviews, research paper series, and papers presented at meetings of scholarly societies). Each issue of *SA*, like that of *Psychological Abstracts,* organizes literature in broad subject classifications. Although *SA* contains a grouping for social psychology (including small groups, leadership, personality, and culture), our primary access to information is through the subject index provided in each issue and in each annual cumulated index.

Beginning with 1986, *SA* relies on the *Thesaurus of Sociological Indexing Terms* as the source of headings used in its subject indexes. It contains some of the same features as the *Thesaurus of Psychological Index Terms,* such as the Alphabetical List of Terms and the Rotated Descriptor Display. The Alphabetical List (see Figure 5–J) includes the term *Stress* in boldface type (**50**), indicating it is a usable subject heading. We also find a list of related terms (RT) (**51**) and narrower terms (NT) (**52**), including the more specific term, *Psychological Stress* (**53**). Checking under *Psychological Stress* in the *Thesaurus* (**53a**), we find that it also has list of related terms and a broader term (BT) (**50a**). Descriptor codes (DC) (**54**), numeric equivalents of *Thesaurus* descriptors, are used primarily for computerized searching of the *Sociological Abstracts* database. References from unacceptable terms to acceptable subject headings are indicated by "Use" references (**55**).

Sociological Abstracts has been published since 1953, but *Thesaurus* terms were not used until 1986. From 1953 to 1985, the subject indexes used key words or phrases as indexing terms. The *Thesaurus* uses *historical notes* to help you use the subject indexes before 1986. In the case of *Stress,* the historical note (HN) (**56**) indicates the term *Stress/Stresses* was used from 1963–1985. A more

FIGURE 5–J

Entries from the *Thesaurus of Sociological Indexing Terms* (2nd ed., 1989, pp. 194, 245).

Psychiatric Social Work
　Use Clinical Social Work

Psychiatric Social Workers
　Use Social Workers

• • •

（53a）——————**Psychological Stress**
　　DC D677400 ————————————（54）
　　HN Formerly (1985) DC 358010.
（50a）——————**BT** Stress
　　RT Anxiety
　　　　Cognitive Dissonance
　　　　Coping
　　　　Occupational Stress
　　　　Psychological Distress
　　　　Psychological Factors
　　　　Tension

• • •

Sterility/Fertility (1966-1985) ————（57）
（55）————**HN** DC 445200
　　Use Childlessness

• • •

（50）——————**Stress**
　　DC D836700
（56）————**HN** Formerly (1963-1985) DC 447000.
　　　　Stress/Stresses.
　　NT Occupational Stress
　　　　Psychological Stress ————————（53）
（52）————**RT** Ambiguity
　　　　Coping
　　　　Crises
（51）————Crowding
　　　　Diseases
　　　　Environment
　　　　Health
　　　　Life Events
　　　　Physiology
　　　　Pressure
　　　　Shock
　　　　Threat

---

significant change occurred in the case of *Sterility/Fertility* (**57**), which was used from 1966 to 1985, for which the acceptable term is now *Childlessness.*

Having identified our subject heading, we begin looking in the subject indexes to *SA.* As the example from the 1988 cumulated index in Figure 5–K indicates, references are represented by phrases that briefly describe the subject content of each article. Under *Psychological Stress* (**53b**), "children's well-being, post-marital dissolution, . . . " (**58**) suggests that this reference may be relevant. Following each identifying phrase is a citation number (**59**), which we use to locate the reference in the main entry section of the corresponding volume of *SA.*

As shown in Figure 5–L, each item in the main entry section begins with the citation number (**59a**), followed by the names of the authors (**60**), the institutional affiliation of the authors (**61**), and the article title (**62**). Bibliographic information provided (**63**) includes

FIGURE 5-K
Subject index entries from *Sociological Abstracts: Cumulative Subject Index* (Vol. 36, 1988, p. 3042).

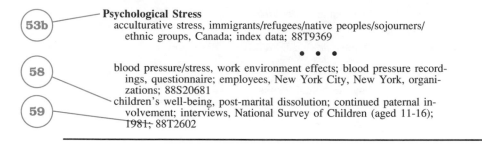

(53b) **Psychological Stress**
acculturative stress, immigrants/refugees/native peoples/sojourners/ ethnic groups, Canada; index data; 88T9369

• • •

(58) blood pressure/stress, work environment effects; blood pressure recordings, questionnaire; employees, New York City, New York, organizations; 88S20681

(59) children's well-being, post-marital dissolution; continued paternal involvement; interviews, National Survey of Children (aged 11-16); 1981; 88T2602

the journal title, the year of publication, the volume and the issue numbers, the month or date of the issue, and the page numbers. The UM symbol **(64)** indicates that a copy of this article is available from the University Microfilms International (UMI) article reproduction service. In addition, an abstract **(65)** summarizes the article.

SA also has an author index. The Source Index arranges citations by the title of the journal in which it appeared. This index also indicates the availability of articles from selected journal titles through reproduction services offered by the publisher, Sociological Abstracts, Inc., or by UMI.

FIGURE 5-L
A partial main entry citation from the Sociology of the Child section in *Sociological Abstracts* (Vol. 36, issue 1, April 1988, p. 201).

(59a) Sociological Abstracts   *THE FAMILY & SOCIALIZATION*   *88T2606*

(60) 88T2602

(61) **Furstenberg, Frank F., Jr., Morgan S. Phillip & Allison, Paul D.** (Dept Sociology U Pennsylvania, Philadelphia 19104-6299), **Paternal Participation and Children's Well-Being after Marital Dissolution,** UM *American Sociological Review,* 1987, 52, 5, Oct, 695--701.   (62)

(64)

(63) ¶ The influence of continued paternal involvement following divorce on children's well-being is investigated using interview data from 227 US children (part of the larger National Survey of Children) aged 11-16 who in 1981 were living with their mothers following their parents' marital dissolution. For measures of academic difficulty, problem behavior, &   (65)

References

Albrecht, K. (1979). *Stress and the manager.* Englewood Cliffs, NJ: Prentice-Hall.

Beech, H. R. (1987). Controlling physiological stress reactions. In R. Kalimo, M. A. El-Batawi, & C. L. Cooper (Eds.), *Psychosocial factors at work and their relation to health* (pp. 206–216). Geneva: World Health Organization.

Cannon, W. B. (1932). *The wisdom of the body.* New York: Norton.

Cohen, S., & Williamson, G. M. (1991). Stress and infectious disease in humans. *Psychological Bulletin, 109,* 5–24.

Cooper, C. L. (1987). Coping with stress in organizations: The role of management. In R. Kalimo, M. A. El-Batawi, & C. L. Cooper (Eds.), *Psychosocial factors at work and their relation to health* (pp. 185–205). Geneva: World Health Organization.

Croog, S. H. (1970). The family as a source of stress. In S. Levine & N. A. Scotch (Eds.), *Social stress* (pp. 19–53). Chicago: Aldine.

Davis, M. D., Eshelman, E. R., & McKay, M. (1988). *The relaxation and stress reduction workbook* (3rd ed.). Oakland, CA: New Harbinger Publications.

Denney, D. R. (1980). Self-control approaches to the treatment of test anxiety. In I. G. Sarason (Ed.), *Test anxiety: Theory, research and applications* (pp. 209–243). Hillsdale, NJ: Lawrence Erlbaum.

Farber, S. L. (1982). Genetic diversity and differing reactions to stress. In L. Goldberger & S. Breznitz (Eds.), *Handbook of stress: Theoretical and clinical aspects* (pp. 123–133). New York: Free Press.

Goldberger, L., & Breznitz, S. (Eds.). (1982). *Handbook of stress: Theoretical and clinical aspects.* New York: Free Press.

Greenberg, J. S. (1983). *Comprehensive stress management.* Dubuque, IA: William C. Brown Company.

Holmes, T. H., & Rahe, R. H. (1967). The Social Readjustment Rating Scale. *Journal of Psychosomatic Research, 11,* 213–218.

Holroyd, K. A., & Lazarus, R. S. (1982). Stress, coping, and somatic adaptation. In L. Goldberger & S. Breznitz (Eds.), *Handbook of stress: Theoretical and clinical aspects* (pp. 21–35). New York: Free Press.

Ivancevich, J. M., & Matteson, M. T. (1980). *Stress and work: A managerial perspective.* Glenview, IL: Scott, Foresman.

Ivancevich, J. M., Matteson, M. T., Freedman, S. M., & Phillips, J. S. (1990). Worksite stress management interventions. *American Psychologist, 45,* 252–261.

Janis, I. L. (1982). Decisionmaking under stress. In L. Goldberger & S. Breznitz (Eds.), *Handbook of stress: Theoretical and clinical aspects* (pp. 69–87). New York: Free Press.

Klarreich, S. H. (1990). *Work without stress.* New York: Brunner/Mazel.

Lazarus, R. S. (1966). *Psychological stress and the coping process.* New York: McGraw-Hill.

Levi, L. (1987). Psychosomatic disease as a consequence of occupational stress. In R. Kalimo, M. S. El-Batawi, & C. L. Cooper (Eds.), *Psychosocial factors at work and their relation to health* (pp. 78–91). Geneva: World Health Organization.

Mandler, G. (1982). Stress and thought processes. In L. Goldberger & S. Breznitz (Eds.), *Handbook of stress: Theoretical and clinical aspects* (pp. 88–104). New York: Free Press.

Mason, L. J. (1985). *Guide to stress reduction.* Berkeley, CA: Celestial Arts.

Rosenman, R. H., & Chesney, M. A. (1982). Stress, Type A behavior, and coronary disease. In L. Goldberger & S. Breznitz (Eds.), *Handbook of stress: Theoretical and clinical aspects* (pp. 547–565). New York: Free Press.

Rosenthal, T. L. (1980). Modeling approaches to test anxiety and related performance problems. In I. G. Sarason (Ed.), *Test anxiety: Theory, research, and applications* (pp. 245–270). Hillsdale, NJ: Erlbaum.

Sarason, I. G. (1978). The Test Anxiety Scale: Concept and research. In C. D. Spielberger & I. G. Sarason (Eds.), *Stress and anxiety* (Vol. 5, pp. 193–215). Washington, DC: Hemisphere.

Sarason, I. G. (1980). Introduction to the study of test anxiety. In I. G. Sarason (Ed.), *Test anxiety: Theory, research, and applications* (pp. 3–14). Hillsdale, NJ: Lawrence Erlbaum.

Sarason, I. G. (1984). Stress, anxiety, and cognitive interference: Reaction to tests. *Journal of Personality and Social Psychology, 46*, 929–938.

Selye, H. (1956). *The stress of life.* New York: McGraw-Hill.

Sieber, J. E. (1980). Defining test anxiety: Problems and approaches. In I. G. Sarason (Ed.), *Test anxiety: Theory, research, and applications* (pp. 15–40). Hillsdale, NJ: Lawrence Erlbaum.

Steptoe, A., & Appels, A. (1989). *Stress, personal control, and health.* New York: John Wiley & Sons.

U.S. Bureau of the Census. (1990). *Statistical abstract of the United States: 1990* (110th ed.). Washington, DC: U.S. Government Printing Office.

U.S. Department of Health, Education, & Welfare. (1967). *1967 annual report* (SuDoc: FS1.1:967). Washington, DC: U.S. Government Printing Office.

Veninga, R. L., & Spradley, J. P. (1981). *The work stress connection.* New York: Ballantine.

Wallerstein, J. S., & Kelley, J. G. (1980). *Surviving the breakup: How children and parents cope with divorce.* New York: Basic Books.

6 The Author/Citation Approach to Searching

Sources Discussed

Social sciences citation index (SSCI). (1969–present). Philadelphia: Institute for Scientific Information. Three times a year. Cumulated annually with multiyear cumulations (1956–1965, 1966–1970, 1971–1975, 1976–1980, 1981–1985).

Science citation index (SCI). (1961, 1964–present). Philadelphia: Institute for Scientific Information. Bimonthly. Cumulatcd annually with multiyear cumulations (1945–1954, 1955–1964, 1965–1969, 1970–1974, 1975–1979, 1980–1984, 1985–1989).

Why Citation Searching?

Original contributions to a field occur as authors report a new finding or offer a new theory that significantly changes understanding of a field, points researchers in a new direction, or initiates a new area of investigation. The intelligence theories discussed in chapter 4 provide an example of such contributions. However, a new line of published research may exist for years without being described by appropriate subject headings in a subject-oriented indexing or abstracting service. Subject indexers may use a variety of indexing terms to identify publications in an emerging area of study. Thus, using a subject search to identify sources relevant to a topic may be difficult.

The citation-searching approach provides you with an alternative to subject searching. To search for citations, you do not need to rely on subject headings, indexing terms, or the judgment of indexers. Citation indexes are based on the premise that published research in an area includes references to previously published papers, which provide the theoretical and empirical context for the new paper. And this premise is based on the assumption that researchers are familiar with the literature in their area and have selected and cited previously published references that are relevant to their own work. If you can identify an important early source in an area, you should be able to identify later articles citing that source.

Chapter Example: Child Aggression

The research of Alfred Bandura and his colleagues on imitative learning of aggressive behavior in children, often remembered for its use of an inflatable "Bobo" doll, has been encountered by many psychology students. To understand why this research was conducted we need to know something about the psychological context of the times as well as Bandura's approach, social learning theory.

In the 1950s, several theories competed for dominance in American psychology as explanations for aggression. One approach was that of psychoanalysis. Sigmund Freud (1948) argued that aggressiveness was instinctive, a manifestation of the death instinct (thanatos), which when turned outward resulted in hostility and destructiveness.

Learning theorists of the period, however, objected to the lack of empirical validation of psychoanalytic explanations. Some attempted to translate psychoanalytic propositions into testable empirical hypotheses of learning theory, such as the frustration–aggression hypothesis (Dollard, Doob, Miller, Mower, & Sears, 1939). The initial approach held that frustration leads to aggression (Dollard et al., 1939); however, later formulations recognized that aggression is only one of several possible responses to frustration, other possibilities including withdrawal, apathy, or increased efforts (Miller, 1941). They also distanced themselves from the position that aggression is innate (Miller & Dollard, 1941).

Operant conditioning (Skinner, 1953) offered another explanation. According to this model, aggressive behavior is learned social behavior. It is shaped through experience with the environment in a series of successive approximations in which the aggressive behaviors are reinforced. Only as responses are emitted, however, and either reinforced or punished, is this behavior learned.

Social learning theory (Bandura, 1977) provided another alternative. While social behavior is learned, there are two ways in which learning occurs—through reinforcement and through imitation. It was argued that aggressive behavior can be acquired through observing and imitating others, without the necessity of reinforcement of the learner's behavior. This was demonstrated in a series of studies.

Bandura, Ross, and Ross (1961) set out to test whether aggressive behavior could be learned through observation. They exposed male and female nursery school children to male and female adults who served as role models. With half of the experimental group subjects, models behaved aggressively toward a 5-foot inflated Bobo doll. The other subjects were exposed to a model behaving nonaggressively. Subjects played briefly with some attractive toys, but were interrupted by the experimenter and told that these toys were for other children (a frustration treatment). Subjects were taken to another room containing toys, including a Bobo doll, and allowed to play. Behavior of each subject was recorded for 20 minutes in this posttreatment observation period. Children exposed to an aggressive model displayed significantly more aggressive behaviors than those exposed to a nonaggressive model, or to children in a control group who received no exposure to a model. It was concluded that social learning can be accomplished by observing a model; and that observation of an adult model communicates acceptance of aggressive behavior, reducing inhibitions on aggression.

Bandura, Ross, and Ross (1963a) used similar procedures and subjects to determine whether film-mediated aggressive models would serve as a source of imitative behavior. Three experimental conditions were used (real-life aggressive models, films of aggressive models, cartoon film aggression) along with a control condition. Children in all three experimental groups displayed significantly more aggressive behavior toward the Bobo doll than children in the control group. Boys tended to display significantly more aggression than girls. The authors concluded that "exposure to filmed aggression heightens aggressive reactions in children" and "pictorial mass media, particularly television, may serve as an important source of social behavior" (p. 9).

Bandura, Ross, and Ross (1963b) used similar procedures. This time, film models were either reinforced or punished for their aggressive behavior. Children who observed films of the rewarded-aggressive model displayed significantly more aggression in a delayed imitation observation period than children who observed the punished-aggressive model. It was concluded that "imitation is partly dependent upon response-consequences to the model" (p. 605).

In a fourth study, Bandura (1965) exposed children to three film conditions: model punished, model rewarded, or no consequence to the model. Following the observation period, the experimenter offered rewards to subjects in all conditions for producing the aggressive behaviors presented in the films. Boys in the punished-model condition and girls in all conditions demonstrated aggressive imitative behaviors. Performance of aggressive behaviors, however, differed based upon observation of reinforcement contingencies on the model's behavior and sex of the subject.

In this chapter, we illustrate the principles of citation searching by using the report of Bandura et al. (1963a) on imitative learning of aggressive behavior through film/television viewing. We are particularly interested in learning what impact this study has had on other areas of research.

Social Sciences Citation Index

Initiated in 1969, the *Social Sciences Citation Index (SSCI)* currently provides complete coverage of about 1,400 journals and selective coverage of approximately 3,300 additional journals in the social sciences. Among the disciplines it covers are anthropology, archaeology, business, communication, psychology, sociology, statistics, and women's studies. It lists articles, editorials, letters, book reviews, conference reports, conference proceedings, and books. *SSCI* does not, however, provide abstracts or detailed contents of the sources covered.

The General Introduction to *SSCI* claims that the index can be used to answer such questions as the following: "Has this paper been cited?" "Has there been a review on this subject?" "Has this work been extended?" "Who else is working in this field?" (*SSCI*, 1989, p. 7). Published three times per year and cumulated annually and quinquennially, *SSCI* contains four basic parts: the Citation Index, the Source Index, the Corporate Index, and the Permuterm Subject Index. A typical *SSCI* annual cumulation is composed of several thousand pages in multiple volumes. A retrospective set covering the years 1956 to 1965 has also been published. A com-

FIGURE 6–A

Entries in the Citation Index of the *Social Sciences Citation Index 1989 Annual* (Vol. 1, 1989, cols. 770, 771, 772), showing recently published articles that have referred to an earlier source by A. Bandura.

Citation Index

(1) **BANDURA A**

• • •

56 J ABNORMAL SOCIAL PS 52 333				
HOLLANDE B	PSYCHOTHER		26	448 89
KELLY KR	J COUN PSYC		36	158 89
• • •				
(2) **63 J ABNORMAL SOCIAL PS 66 3**				
HEATH L	ARCH G PSYC	R	46	376 89
(3) NIKKEN P	J BROADC EL		32	441 88
WIDOM CS	PSYCHOL B	R	106	3 89
WRIGHT JC	J COMM		39	27 89
• • •				
77 PSYCHOL REV 84 191				
SEE SCI FOR 6 ADDITIONAL CITATIONS (4)				
AMBUHL H	PSY PSY MED		39	1 89
ARNKOFF DB	CLIN PSYCH		9	61 89
AUERBACH SM	J CONS CLIN	R	57	388 89
AYERS TD	AM J ORTHOP		59	215 89

panion series, begun in 1963, is *Science Citation Index (SCI)*, which covers literature in the natural sciences. Retrospective sets extend coverage of *SCI* back to 1945.

Using *SSCI*

Searching *SSCI* begins with an accurate citation to an important early primary source. In our search, the complete citation is "Imitation of film-mediated aggressive models" by Albert Bandura, Dorothea Ross, and Sheila R. Ross, *Journal of Abnormal and Social Psychology,* 1963, Volume 66, pages 3–11. For the purpose of illustration we begin with a recent annual cumulation of *SSCI*. As the search progresses, we both work backward in time to earlier volumes and check more recent uncumulated paper issues.

We turn first to the Citation Index in *SSCI*. This section is arranged alphabetically by cited author. If an author has more than one citation, the entries are listed below his or her name chronologically by year of publication. Figure 6–A presents a segment of the 1989 *SSCI* annual cumulation showing entries for the first author, Albert Bandura (**1**). Scanning the list, we find "63 J ABNORMAL SOCIAL PS 66 3" (**2**), an abbreviated citation to the original reference, including (in order) the year of publication, the journal title, the volume number, and the number of the first page of the article. Following this information, in alphabetical order by author, is a list of sources included in this edition of *SSCI* that have cited the Bandura, Ross, and Ross (1963a) reference. One of these is an article by P. Nikken (**3**) appearing in *Journal of Broadcasting and Electronic Media* (J BROADC EL), Volume 32, starting on page 441 in 1988. In some cases, *SSCI* will refer to additional citations in its companion publication, *Science Citation Index* (**4**).

To learn more about the Nikken reference, we turn to the Source Index of *SSCI*, illustrated in Figure 6–B. Listed in this index are all

FIGURE 6–B

Entries in the Source Index of *Social Sciences Citation Index 1989 Annual* (Vol. 5, 1989, col. 7830), providing complete bibliographic information on an article by P. Nikken, including the sources referenced.

BANDURA A	63 J ABNORMAL SOCIAL PS	66	3	
DONOHUE WA	77 HUM RELAT	30	609	
DORR A	83 CHILDRENS UNDERSTAND		199	
HAWKINS RP	77 COMMUNICATION RES	4	299	
KORZENNY F	76 APR INT COMM ASS CON			
LEVELT PBM	84 SESAMSTRAAT MILIEU			
MESSARIS P	83 COMMUN RES	10	175	
NIKKEN P	84 THESIS STATE U UTREC			
PINGREE S	78 PSYCHOL WOMEN Q	2	262	
POTTER WJ	81 DEV INSTRUMENT MEASU			
"	88 J BROADCAST ELECTRON	32	23	
REEVES B	78 JOURNALISM QUART	55	682	
"	78 "	55	695	
VANDERVOORT THA	86 TELEVISION VIOLENCE			

of the articles, books, and other documents included in the 1989 edition, arranged in alphabetical order by author. We find P. Nikken (**3a**) listed in Volume 5, column 7830. Then we locate the entry for J BROADC EL (**5**). The title of the article that appears in this journal is listed above (**6**), and it indicates that the article expands Bandura's research to how children perceive and interpret television reality. The citation further elaborates on the information we obtained from the Citation Index: Nikken's article was coauthored with A. L. Peeters (**7**), it appears in the fourth issue of Volume 32 (**8**) of *Journal of Broadcasting and Electronic Media*, is 12 pages long (**9**), was published in 1988 (**10**), and includes a total of 14 references (**11**). The entry also indicates Nikken's address at the time this article was published (**12**). Following this information, in alphabetical order by author, is a list of the 14 sources cited by Nikken in this article. The first is the Bandura et al. (1963a) article (**2a**) with which we began.

If you were to expand this search, you might include related articles by Bandura listed in the Citation Index. You would have to consult both previous and later editions of *SSCI* for references published in other years.

Other Features of *SSCI*

The Permuterm Subject Index provides a kind of subject access to *SSCI* materials. Unlike other indexes we have examined, this *keyword index* does not depend upon the judgment of professional indexers or upon a controlled vocabulary. Generated and produced by computer, it lists as subject entries significant words in article titles. Entries for the Nikken article therefore appear under *children's, perceptions, reality,* and *television* in the Permuterm Index. A subject search with this index may be useful if you are interested in a broad range of publications from many social science disciplines. However, if an article's title does not accurately indicate its subject content, you will probably overlook the article. Furthermore, the Permuterm Subject Index does not identify related articles. Therefore you could not use it to uncover the relationship between the Nikken and Bandura articles that we found using the author/citation approach.

The Corporate Index contains two sections: geographic and organizational. Citations in the geographic section are arranged by the organizational locations of the authors and their institutional affiliations. For example, knowing (from the *SSCI* Source Index) that Nikken was at the Foundation for Childrens Well Being when his article was published, you might wish to learn what other research has been reported by persons at that location. The organizational section acts as an index to the index described above, listing institutions under their names and providing their geographic locations.

The List of Source Publications includes both the full title and the abbreviation for each journal covered in an edition of *SSCI*. The list is included in each cumulation of *SSCI*. We used it to decipher the abbreviations J ABNORMAL SOCIAL PS and J BROADC EL. You should consult the list for the accurate, complete title or the appropriate abbreviation for each journal identified. Because more than 4,000 different journals are indexed in each edition of *SSCI*, abbreviations for many journals are similar. Attempting to locate an incorrect journal title can be time-consuming and frustrating.

Each annual edition of *SSCI* includes an extensive introduction and guide providing further information about many features of *SSCI* and *SCI*. The introduction also includes historical information on the development of citation indexing, research on citation indexing, and research on patterns of scientific citation.

Incidentally, *SSCI* and *SCI* are extremely expensive indexes. Although they provide unique coverage of literature in the social and natural sciences, they are too expensive for many smaller libraries. Thus, to use this tool you may need to visit a library other than the one you usually use. A reference librarian may be able to direct you to libraries that have these indexes.

References

Bandura, A. (1965). Influence of models' reinforcement contingencies on the acquisition of imitative responses. *Journal of Personality and Social Psychology, 1,* 589–595.

Bandura, A. (1977). *Social learning theory.* Englewood Cliffs, NJ: Prentice-Hall.

Bandura, A., Ross, D., & Ross, S. A. (1961). Transmission of aggression through imitation of aggressive models. *Journal of Abnormal and Social Psychology, 63,* 575–582.

Bandura, A., Ross, D., & Ross, S. A. (1963a). Imitation of film mediated aggressive models. *Journal of Abnormal and Social Psychology, 66,* 3–11.

Bandura, A., Ross, D., & Ross, S. A. (1963b). Vicarious reinforcement and imitative learning. *Journal of Abnormal and Social Psychology, 67,* 601–607.

Dollard, J., Doob, L., Miller, N. E., Mower, O., & Sears, R. (1939). *Frustration and aggression.* New Haven, CT: Yale University Press.

Freud, S. (1948). *Beyond the pleasure principle* (C. J. M. Hubback, Trans.). London: Hogarth Press.

Miller, N. E. (1941). An experimental investigation of acquired drives. *Psychological Bulletin, 38,* 534–535.

Miller, N. E., & Dollard, J. (1941). *Social learning and imitation.* New Haven, CT: Yale University Press.

Skinner, B. F. (1953). *Science and human behavior.* New York: Free Press.

7 Government Publications

Sources Discussed

U.S. Superintendent of Documents. (1895–present). *Monthly catalog of United States government publications.* Washington, DC: U.S. Government Printing Office. Monthly.

Index to U.S. government periodicals. (1970–present). Chicago: Infordata International. Quarterly; cumulated annually.

Library of Congress. Exchange and Gifts Division. (1910–present). *Monthly checklist of state publications.* Washington, DC: U.S. Goverment Printing Office. Monthly.

National Technical Information Service. *Government reports announcements & index.* (1946–present). Springfield, VA: National Technical Information Service. Bimonthly.

United Nations. Dag Hammarskjold Library. (1950–present). *UNDOC: Current Index; United Nations document index.* New York: United Nations. Monthly.

What Are Government Publications?

Government publications include materials issued by local, state, regional, federal, foreign, or international governmental organizations. Issuing agencies may be part of an executive, legislative, or judicial branch, or they may be independent regulatory agencies. Publications are produced in every size from a single page to a multivolume set and are available on almost any topic imaginable.

In this chapter we focus attention primarily upon publications of the United States federal government. These publications are widely distributed and available throughout the United States. The federal government, through the U.S. Government Printing Office (GPO), is the largest single publisher in the United States and one of the largest in the world. In 1989, the GPO operated government bookstores in 23 cities around the United States and distributed 27 million copies of 68,000 titles to 1,396 depository libraries (U.S. GPO, 1990). In 1989, almost 2 million orders for sales were processed, approximately 99 million publications were distributed, and 27 thousand documents were cataloged (U.S. GPO, 1990).

State, local, and international publications are less widely distributed and less accessible. Therefore we mention them briefly.

We cover government publications in a separate chapter for several reasons. The vast majority of publications issued by government bodies are not covered by the various abstracting and indexing services discussed in chapters 4, 5, and 6. A variety of separate indexes provide access to government publications. Also, many libraries having a sizable collection of government publications handle these materials separately from other library materials.

The Depository Library Program

Almost 1,400 college, university, government, special, and public libraries in the United States have been designated as *Federal Depository Libraries.* Depositories are eligible to receive more than 7,200 classes of publications free of charge. These libraries are operated according to the provisions of the *Guidelines for the Depository Library System* (U.S. GPO, 1988).

Each federal congressional district is eligible for two depository libraries designated by members of the House of Representatives and each state may contain one or two others designated by senators (U.S. GPO, 1988). According to the *Guidelines,*

> The purpose of depository libraries is to make U.S. Government publications easily accessible to the general public and to insure their continued availability in the future. . . . depository libraries will receive free Federal public documents. . . . The library shall be open to the general public for the free use of depository publications. . . . Each library should acquire and maintain the basic catalogs, guides and indexes, retrospective and current, considered essential to the reference use of the collection. Each depository should select frequently used and potentially useful materials appropriate to the objectives of the library. (U.S. GPO, 1988, pp. 3, 5–6)

Depository libraries receive, on a daily basis, shipments of publications in any series that they've requested.

Nondepository libraries and individuals may purchase numerous federal government publications. These publications may be ordered from sources such as the following: *U.S. Government Books,* published bimonthly and listing about 1,000 publications in each issue; *Subject Bibliographies,* listing federal government publications in over 300 different areas such as alcoholism, child abuse, family planning, juvenile delinquency, mental health, occupational safety, reading, vocational education, and women; and the *Monthly Catalog,* which we discuss in this chapter.

Chapter Example: Aging

In this chapter, we focus on the the psychology of aging. Several primary questions may be asked. What is aging? What happens during the aging process? What are the consequences of changes during aging? How can people respond to aging changes?

Birren and Cunningham (1985) suggest that for many psychologists, the fundamental question in the psychology of aging has shifted from "How does behavior become organized?" to "How does behavior change as we age?" They have defined aging as "regular changes that occur in mature genetically representative organisms living under representative environmental conditions." (Birren & Cunningham, 1985, p. 5)

There appear to be three primary components of aging as an individual passes from young adulthood through middle age and into old age: biological aging, sociological aging, and psychological aging. In biological aging (senescence), changes take place in an individual's functional capacities along with increasing physical vulnerability. In sociological aging (eldering), the individual faces and adapts to societal expectations of changed social roles, habits, and status consistent with one's age. In psychological aging (geronting), individuals choose to behave in a variety of ways as they adapt to biological and sociological aging (Birren & Birren, 1990).

Changes during the transition from midlife to old age involve growth as well as decline (Baltes, 1987; Heckhousen, Dixon & Baltes, 1989). Much reporting has focused on the decline that may occur.

The nervous system is a limiting factor in the aging process. It is critical in the organization of behavior, physiological functioning, and combating disease. As aging processes occur, biological aging and resulting somatic disorders may affect an individual's quality of life (Elias, Elias, & Elias, 1990).

Changes in physical health may include visual impairment due to glaucoma or cataracts (Kline & Schieber, 1985) or decreased hearing due to reduction in absolute sensitivity to sound (Olsho, Harkins, & Lenhardt, 1985). Changes in cognition can include memory decrements of various types (Poon, 1985) and reduced problem solving capabilities (Reese & Rodeheaver, 1985). Aging has also been linked to an increased incidence of mental illness due to depression and dementia (Cohen, 1990).

Physical declines in areas such as those noted above, however, are not inevitable. Positive experiences that may occur include development of wisdom and practical intelligence, experience of personal fulfillment, social gains in retirement, and remembering (Baltes, 1987; Fozard, 1980; Whitbourne & Hulicka, 1990). Skinner's (1983) personal account offers anecdotal information about changes involving both growth and loss.

What kinds of support are available, and can they be of benefit to those in need of assistance? Rehabilitation services of various types are offered in different communities with varying success rates in combating biological aging. Among other things, motivation to participate and family involvement appear to be critical mediators of success in rehabilitation (Kemp, 1985). Interventions have included home health care and nutritional programs such as Meals on Wheels. A variety of psychological interventions have been attempted to facilitate positive psychological aging, including individual therapy, family counseling, pet therapy, group therapy, and recreation therapy. A variety of social support services have attempted to respond to sociological and psychological problems in aging, including case management. Many older persons can also be aided by careful design and adaptation of residential environments. This is critical to support independence and maximize the quality of life (Lawton, 1990).

The government is an abundant source of information on research on the aging process itself as well as on the consequences of aging. As a sponsor of many programs serving the elderly, the government provides information on mental health treatment, social rehabilitation, health care, housing, and other support programs. And as an entity which creates laws, the government is a source of data on aging and social policy.

In this chapter, we discuss mechanisms for locating government publications. Our focus is on documents related to the topic of aging. Of course, an actual search would involve a much narrower, focused topic, with a documents search supplementing other materials found in a catalog of books and journal indexes. However, we will keep our discussion broad enough to illustrate the breadth of government publishing and the wealth of information available. The most important questions at this point are, how are the publications of the federal agencies organized, and how can we locate these publications?

Organization of Government Publications

Many nondepository libraries order, receive, catalog, and arrange government publications in the same way they do materials from commercial publishers. For example, nondepository libraries may catalog and shelve government monographs with other books, government periodicals with other library periodicals, and selected materials of special importance with the general library collection. Depository libraries receive so many government publications, however, that these libraries tend to handle such publications separately from other library materials.

Most depository libraries organize documents according to the Superintendent of Documents Classification number system (SuDoc). The SuDoc system is an alphanumeric notation system. Let us examine the SuDoc number for a typical publication, *Aging in the Eighties* (SuDoc number HE 20.6209/3:124), issued by the

TABLE 7-A

Analysis of a Superintendent of Documents Classification System (SuDoc) Number (HE 20.6209/3:124)

Class stem	HE	Parent agency	Department of Health & Human Services
	20	Subagency	Public Health Service
	6201–6519		National Center for Health Statistics, Vital and Health Statistics
	6209/3	Series	Advance data from the Vital & Health Statistics
Book number	124	Publication	*Aging in the Eighties, Age 65 Years and Over—Use of Community Services*

Department of Health and Human Services. Table 7-A explains this SuDoc number. The letters at the beginning indicate the parent department or agency. Departments and agencies are subdivided into bureaus, offices, and agencies, indicated by numbers. In this case, a particular publication series is identified following a slash mark. A colon then precedes the number identifying the particular publication.

In the SuDoc system, as illustrated in Table 7-B, publications are organized by issuing agency. (Notice from the table that there are several agencies of potential interest to psychologists.) Thus two publications on the same topic by different agencies would be located in different places, whereas two publications on radically different topics by the same agency are arranged in alphanumeric order together. This system is difficult to manage partly because the federal government is extremely large and partly because governmental reorganization changes the numbering system. For example, educational materials have been issued by the Education Bureau in the Interior Department (code I16), transferred to the Federal Security Agency (code FS), which became the Department of Health, Education and Welfare, later known as Department of Health and Human Services (code HE). In 1979, a separate cabinet-level Department of Education was created (code ED). Thus, to avoid confusion and to locate relevant publications, you must rely on indexes.

Monthly Catalog of United States Government Publications

The primary index to federal government publications is the *Monthly Catalog of United States Government Publications (Monthly Catalog)*, issued by the U.S. Superintendent of Documents. First issued in 1895, this index has since endured several changes of title and structure. In 1976 the *Monthly Catalog* adopted its present format. Currently, cataloging and indexing follow the same rules that the Library of Congress uses in cataloging books (see chapter 3). Prior to 1976, the *Monthly Catalog* used its own system, which many librarians believe was incomplete and difficult to use.

TABLE 7–B

Organization of Issuing-Agency Prefix Codes for Selected Agencies in the Superintendent of Documents (SuDoc) Classification System

SuDoc Code	Agency
CR	Civil Rights Commission
ED	Department of Education
HE	Department of Health & Human Services
HE 3	Social Security Administration
HE 20	Public Health Service
HE 20.3000	National Institutes of Health
HE 20.3851-3868	National Institute on Aging
HE 20.8000	Alcohol, Drug Abuse, and Mental Health Administration
HE 20.8100	National Institute of Mental Health
HE 22	Health Care Financing Administration
HE 23	Office of Human Development Services
HE 23.100	President's Committee on Mental Retardation
HE 23.3000	Administration on Aging
HE 23.3100	National Clearinghouse on Aging
HH	Department of Housing & Urban Development
L	Department of Labor
Y 3.F31/15	Federal Council on Aging
Y 3.W58/4	White House Conference on Aging
Y 4.Ag4	Senate. Special Committee on Aging
Y 4.Ag4/2	House. Select Committee on Aging

Each issue of the *Monthly Catalog* contains a description of new documents processed during that monthly period. Publications are arranged alphabetically by agency in each issue. There are seven monthly indexes: author, title, subject, series/report, contract number, stock number, and title key word. Some are cumulated semiannually and annually. Each year a special *Periodicals Supplement* is published listing publications issued three or more times per year.

Using the *Monthly Catalog*

Searching for publications on aging provides an illustration of use of the *Monthly Catalog*. Since the July 1976 issue, the *Monthly Catalog* uses *Library of Congress Subject Headings* as the source of its controlled vocabulary (see chapter 3). Therefore, you may begin by using the LC subject headings for searching in the *Monthly Catalog* Subject Index. Figure 7–A presents several Subject Index (1) entries from the annual Cumulative Index for 1985. Notice the subject headings used are in boldface type and include both *Aged* (2) (the population of elderly persons) and *Aging* (3) (the process of aging). Under these general subject headings are more specific subject subdivisions, such as *Aged—United States—Social conditions* (4) and *Aging—Statistics* (5). Although many of the items concern aging in the population and focus on the elderly population, the

FIGURE 7-A

Subject Index entries for publications on aging from the Cumulative Index to the *Monthly Catalog of U.S. Government Publications* (Vol. III, p. I-1387), 1985.

Subject Index

(1)

(4) **Aged — United States — Social conditions.**
Cultural programs for and by older adults : a catalogue of program profiles /, 85-25139

High technology and its benefits for an aging population : hearing before the Select Committee on Aging, House of Representatives, Ninety-eighth Congress, second session, May 22, 1984., 85-3857

Technology and aging in America, 85-23885

Technology and aging in America : summary., 85-9403

(2) **Aged — United States — Statistics.**
America in transition : an aging society, 1984-85 edition : an information paper /, 85-20090

• • •

(3) **Aging.**
(6) Normal human aging : the Baltimore longitudinal study of aging /, 85-17372 **(7)**

The politicization of the 1981 White House Conference on Aging : a report /, 85-3858

U.S. perspectives : international action on aging : a background paper /, 85-16151

Aging — Research — United States — Periodicals.
Special report on aging /, 85-17373

(5) **Aging — Statistics.**
International trends and perspectives : aging /, 85-9698

publication "Normal Human Aging" (**6**), entry number 85-17372 (**7**) appears to emphasize aging as a process. The entry number is unique and indicates the year of cataloging (85) and a number representing a particular item (17372).

To learn more about this publication, we turn to issues of the 1985 *Monthly Catalog*. Entries are numbered sequentially within each annual volume, beginning with entry 1 in January of each year. Entry 85-17372 is shown in Figure 7-B. The boldface heading for the National Institute on Aging (**8**) precedes all entries for this agency. Document descriptions begin with the entry number (**9**). The SuDoc number (**10**), essential for locating the publication in a depository library, is HE 20.3852:B 21/2. This entry lists the title, "Normal Human Aging: The Baltimore Longitudinal Study of Aging"

FIGURE 7–B

Information provided for government publications included in the *Monthly Catalog of U.S. Government Publications* (August 1985, p. 120).

Government Publications — August 1985

⑧ — **NATIONAL INSTITUTE ON AGING**
Health and Human Services Dept.
Bethesda, MD 20014 ⑩

⑨ 85-17372

HE 20.3852:B 21/2

⑪ Normal human aging : the Baltimore longitudinal study of aging / Nathan W. Shock... [et al.] — [Baltimore, Md.] : U.S. Dept. ⑫ of Health and Human Services, Public Health Service, National Institutes of Health, National Institute on Aging, Gerontology Research Center ; Washington, D.C. : For sale by ⑭ the Supt. of Docs., U.S. G.P.O., 1984. ⑬

xix, 399, [34] p. : ill. ; 26 cm.— (NIH publication ; no. 84-⑮ 2450) "November, 1984." Includes bibliographies and index. ●Item 447-A-13 S/N 017-062-00135-9 @ GPO ⑯ 18.00

1. Aging. I. Shock, Nathan Wetherill, 1906- II. Geron⑰ tology Research Center (U.S.) III. Title: The Baltimore longitudinal study of aging. IV. Series: DHHS publication ; no. (NIH) 84-2450. OCLC 11828448 ⑱

③ₐ ⑫ₐ ⑲

(**11**) by Nathan W. Shock and others (**12**). It was published in Baltimore, Maryland, by the Gerontology Research Center (**13**). The volume was published in 1984 and can be purchased from the Superintendent of Documents (**14**).

Descriptive notes indicate that this document contains 399 pages (and some unnumbered pages) of text, has illustrations, is part of the National Institutes of Health Publication series dated November 1984, and contains bibliographies and an index (**15**). The bullet (**16**) indicates that this item is available to depository libraries selecting this series as Item 447-A-13. A copy may be purchased for $18 from GPO as stock number S/N 017-062-00135-9 (**17**).

Following this information are tracings (see chapter 3), which indicate all the ways this document is indexed. As we discovered previously, the document is entered in the Subject Index under *Aging* (**3a**). The Author Index contains an entry for the primary author (**12a**). Additional index entries enable you to locate this book by agency, by title and subtitle, and by publication series (**18**). Because cataloging and indexing have been done since 1976 with the computerized systems of the Online Computer Library Center (OCLC), the *Monthly Catalog* also provides this reference (**19**).

Figure 7–C illustrates several of the index entries. In the Title Index, entry 85-17372 appears under its title (**11a**) and in the Author Index it appears under the primary author's name (**12b**). A

FIGURE 7–C

Index entries for publication 85-17372 from the 1985 Cumulative Index to the *Monthly Catalog of U.S. Government Publications* (Vol. I, pp. I-1160, I-441 and Vol. III, p. I-3011, I-3087, I-3579, I-3704), showing the title entries in the Title Index, an author entry in the Author Index, and entries in the Title Keyword Index.

Title Index

(11a)——— Normal human aging : the Baltimore longitudinal study of aging /,   85-17372

A normal incidence, high resolution x-ray telescope for solar coronal observations : semiannual progress report no. 3, for the period 1 November 1983 through 30 April 1984 microform /,   85-3570

Author Index

Shock and Vibration Information Center.
The Shock and vibration digest : a publication of the Shock and Vibration Information Center, Naval Research Laboratory.,   85-620

(12b)——— **Stock, Nathan Wetherill, 1906-**
Normal human aging : the Baltimore longitudinal study of aging /,   85-17372

Title Keyword Index

Aggregating available soil water-holding capacity	85-15637	
Aging.	85-1102	
" /, A Directory of state and area agencies on	85-18628	
" /, International trends and perspectives :	85-9698	
" /, Normal human aging : the Baltimore longit	85-17372	
" /, Special report on	85-17373	
" ;, Developments in	85-5893	
" ;, Developments in	**85-6145**	
" : report (to accompany S. Res. 45), Authoriz	85-5850	
" : strategies for action /, Health promotion	85-10594	
" :, Summary of states' issues on	85-18629	
" :, Technology and the	85-5627	
" : the Baltimore longitudinal study of aging	85-17372	

(23)

Baltimore and Ohio Railroad Company—control—Detroi	85-2121	
" longitudinal study of aging /, Normal hu	85-17372	
" metropolitan area, Maryland /, Analysis	85-25185	

(22)

longitudinal aerodynamic characteristics of a vect	85-3584	
" aerodynamic characteristics of two fi	85-5344	

" study of aging /, Normal human aging	85-17372	
" study of coherence in children's writ	**85-4463**	
" study of student change in cognitive	85-14511	

(21)

normal development and hatch of embryos of Paratan	85-3033	
" human aging : the Baltimore longitudinal st	85-17372	

(20)

feature of the *Monthly Catalog*, initiated in 1980, is the Title Key-word Index. This index lists entries under important words selected from the document title and subtitle. In this index, publication number 85-17372 appears under the key words *normal* (**20**), *longi-tudinal* (**21**), *Baltimore* (**22**), and twice under the word *aging* (**23**).

To develop an effective subject-search strategy, you begin with relevant descriptors in the most recent issues of the Subject and Title Keyword Indexes and work backward in time to older vol-umes. Because prior to 1976 the *Monthly Catalog* used its own list of subject-indexing terms, your challenge is to identify terms under which relevant publications were indexed. Subject-indexing terms for publications on aging have included aged, elderly, gerontology, old age, older Americans, and senior citizens. Cumulated indexes are available for the periods 1951–1960, 1961–1965, 1966–1970, 1971–1976, 1976–1980, 1981–1985, and 1900–1971. Their em-phasis is on subject indexing.

Continuing a search on aging would uncover numerous addi-tional publications. Several illustrations of what you might find are

TABLE 7–C

Sampling of the Publications on Aging Issued by Various Federal Agencies

SuDoc Number	Issuing Agency	Publication Title
C3.186: P23/128	Census Bureau	*America in Transition: An Aging Society* (1983)
E3.26/4: 0220	Energy Department	*A Comparison of Energy Expenditures by Elderly & Non-Elderly Households— 1975 & 1985* (1980)
GP 3.22/2: O39/990	Superintendent of Documents	*Subject Bibliography: Aging* (1990)
HE 20.3031: B73/2	National Institutes of Health	*Brain in Aging and Dementia* (1983)
HE 23.3002: Su7	Administration on Aging	*National Survey of the Aged* (1982)
HH 1.2: L95/3	Housing & Urban Development Department	*Low Rise Housing for Older People: Behavioral Criteria for Design* (1977)
J1.8/2: Se5	Law Enforcement Assistance Administration	*Crime Prevention Handbook for Senior Citizens* (1977)
Y 3.T 22/2:2 M 66/2	Office of Technology Assessment. Congress.	*Losing a Million Minds: Confronting the Tragedy of Alzheimer's Disease and Other Dementias* (1987)
Y 4.Ag4: Ag 4/9	Special Committee on Aging. Senate	*Aging and the Work Force: Human Resource Strategies* (1982)
Y 4.Ag4/2: El 2/27	Select Committee on Aging. House	*Elder Abuse (An Examination of a Hidden Problem). Staff Report.* (1981)

presented in Table 7–C. For each sample publication, the SuDoc number, the issuing agency, the title, and publication year are listed.

U.S. Government Periodicals

Agencies of the federal government issue over 1,000 different periodicals. These publications are not indexed in the *Monthly Catalog,* and many are not covered in the indexing or abstracting services discussed elsewhere in this book. The *Index to U.S. Government Periodicals,* published quarterly and cumulated annually, covers a selection of these materials. In 1987 it provided access to 170 federal government periodicals by author and subject. At present, the earliest available volume covers materials published in 1970.

Figure 7–D shows several entries on aging from the 1983 *Index.* One article of possible interest is "Brief Cognitive Rating Scale (BCRS): findings in primary degenerative dementia (PDD)" (**24**), written by Barry Reisberg and others (**25**). It appeared in the quarterly journal, *Psychopharmacology Bulletin,* Volume 19, issue 1, on pages 47–50 (**26**). To order a copy of the article you would use the microfiche identifying number, 091. To decipher any abbreviations in the entry you should check the key to abbreviations printed in the front of each volume.

There are many federal government periodicals that may be of interest to psychologists. These include *Aging, American Education, Children Today, Monthly Labor Review, Schizophrenia Bulletin,* and *Social Security Bulletin.*

Other Sources

Materials discussed in the remainder of this chapter may be unavailable in many libraries. We note these sources, however, to complete our discussion and to give you an idea of the variety of publications in existence.

FIGURE 7–D

Listings for publications on aging in the *Index to U.S. Government Periodicals* (1983, p. 28).

INDEX TO U.S. GOVERNMENT PERIODICALS

AGING

Adversity may equip low-income black women to cope well in old age. il Aging 339 40-42 My-Je **83-002**

Aged mice may be more susceptible to infection . . . il, ref Research R Rep 7 3 12-13 Mr **83-278**

Aging of the U.S. population: human resource implications. Malcolm H. Morrison, ref, tab Mon Labor Rev 106 5 13-19 My **83-069**

Antidementia drugs. Thomas Crook, ref Psychopharm Bul 19 1 69-71 **83-091**

Basal forebrain holds clues to Alzheimer's disease. il News & Feat Nih 4-5 Ap **83-300**

Brief Cognitive Rating Scale (BCRS): findings in primary degenerative dementia (PDD). Barry Reisberg and others, tab Psychopharm Bul 19 1 47-50 **83-091**

Changing older population. Donald Fowles, il, gr Aging 339 6-11 My-Je **83-002**

Dietary effects on aging studied in monkey colony. il, ref Research R Rep 7 6 5-7 Je **83-278**

State documents. Agencies in each state in the United States issue a variety of publications. Few libraries have large collections of anything other than their own state's publications. The source that provides the most comprehensive coverage of these materials is the *Monthly Checklist of State Publications,* compiled by the Library of Congress. Published monthly for more than 70 years (with subject indexes that cumulate annually), the *Checklist* provides a record of state documents received at the Library of Congress. The checklist depends on the goodwill and cooperation of many state agencies, which voluntarily forward materials to the Library of Congress. Consequently, it is not a complete list of all state publications. Some states also issue their own checklists.

Unpublished technical reports. Each year thousands of research, development, and technical reports are written. Many of these are prepared under requirements of grants or contracts with federal government agencies; others are prepared for state or local governmental agencies. Similar to materials included in ERIC's *RIE* (see chapter 5), these reports are often reproduced and distributed in a limited fashion. The National Technical Information Service (NTIS) indexes and abstracts them in *Government Reports Announcements and Index.* Some libraries receive selected documents on microfiche in the same way that they receive ERIC microfiche indexed in *RIE.* In addition, copies of most documents may be purchased from NTIS in paper or in microfiche.

United Nations publications. These publications are indexed in *UNDOC: Current Index,* prepared by the Dag Hammarskjold Library. This index is issued 10 times a year, with annual cumulations and indexes. Like the U.S. federal government, the United Nations issues thousands of reports annually. As in the case of state documents and technical reports, however, these publications are often difficult to obtain.

Further information. Given the limitations of space available in this chapter, we have covered only the most highly visible sources and those that we judge to be most widely available in college libraries. For additional information, you should consult a reference librarian or government documents librarian. If you are interested in exploring this area further, the best general guidebook with which we are familiar is Morehead's (1983) *Introduction to United States Public Documents.* Other sources that you may find useful are Andriot's (1990) *Guide to U.S. Government Publications* and Palic's (1975) *Government Publications: A Guide to Bibliographic Tools.*

References

Andriot, D. (Ed.). (1990). *Guide to U.S. government publications.* McLean, VA: Documents Index.

Baltes, P. B. (1987). Theoretical propositions of life-span developmental psychology: On the dynamics between growth and decline. *Developmental Psychology, 23,* 611–626.

Birren, J. E., & Birren, B. A. (1990). The concepts, models, and history of the psychology of aging. In J. E. Birren & K. W. Schaie (Eds.), *Handbook of the psychology of aging* (3rd ed.) (pp. 3–20). San Diego, CA: Academic.

Birren, J. E., & Cunningham, W. (1985). Research on the psychology of aging: Principles, concepts, and theory. In J. E. Birren & K. W. Schaie (Eds.), *Handbook of the psychology of aging* (2nd ed.) (pp. 3–30). New York: Van Nostrand Reinhold.

Cohen, G. D. (1990). Psychopathology and mental health in the mature and elderly adult. In J. E. Birren & K. W. Schaie (Eds.), *Handbook of the psychology of aging* (3rd ed.) (pp. 359–371). San Diego, CA: Academic.

Elias, M. F., Elias, J. W., & Elias, P. K. (1990). Biological and health influences on behavior. In J. E. Birren & K. W. Schaie (Eds.), *Handbook of the psychology of aging* (3rd ed.) (pp. 79–102). San Diego, CA: Academic.

Fozard, J. L. (1980). The time for remembering. In L. W. Poon (Ed.), *Aging in the 1980s: Psychological issues* (pp. 273–287). Washington, DC: American Psychological Association.

Heckhousen, J., Dixon, R. A., & Baltes, P. B. (1989). Gain and losses in development throughout adulthood as perceived by different adult age groups. *Developmental Psychology, 25,* 109–121.

Kemp, B. (1985). Rehabilitation of the old adult. In J. E. Birren & K. W. Schaie (Eds.), *Handbook of the psychology of aging* (2nd ed.) (pp. 647–663). New York: Van Nostrand Reinhold.

Kline, D. W., Schieber, F. (1985). Vision and aging. In J. E. Birren & K. W. Schaie (Eds.), *Handbook of the psychology of aging* (2nd ed.) (pp. 296–331). New York: Van Nostrand Reinhold.

Lawton, M. P. (1990). Residential environment and self-directedness among older people. *American Psychologist, 45,* 638–640.

Morehead, J. (1983). *Introduction to United States public documents.* (3rd ed.). Littleton, CO: Libraries Unlimited.

Olsho, L. W., Harkins, S. W., & Lenhardt, M. L. (1985). Aging and the auditory system. In J. E. Birren & K. W. Schaie (Eds.), *Handbook of the psychology of aging* (2nd ed.) (pp. 332–377). New York: Van Nostrand Reinhold.

Palic, V. M. (1975). *Government publications: A guide to bibliographic tools* (4th ed.). Washington, DC: Library of Congress.

Poon, L. W. (1985). Differences in human memory with aging: Nature, causes, and clinical implications. In J. E. Birren & K. W. Schaie (Eds.), *Handbook of the psychology of aging* (2nd ed.) (pp. 427–464). New York: Van Nostrand Reinhold.

Reese, H. W., & Rodeheaver, D. (1985). Problem solving and complex decision making. In J. E. Birren & K. W. Schaie (Eds.), *Handbook of the psychology of aging* (2nd ed.) (pp. 474–499). New York: Van Nostrand Reinhold.

Skinner, B. F. (1983). Intellectual self-management in old age. *American Psychologist, 38,* 239–244.

U.S. Government Printing Office. (1990). *Annual report 1989* (SuDoc GP 1.1:989). Washington, DC: Author.

U.S. Government Printing Office. (1988). *Guidelines for the depository library system (revised 1987).* Washington, DC: Author.

Whitbourne, S. K., & Hulicka, I. M. (1990). Ageism in undergraduate psychology texts. *American Psychologist, 45,* 1127–1136.

8 The Computer Search

Sources Discussed

Thesaurus of psychological index terms (6th ed.). (1991). Washington, DC: American Psychological Association.

North American online directory. (1985–present). New York: Bowker. Biennial.

Computer-readable databases: A directory and data sourcebook (7th ed.). (1991). Detroit, MI: Gale Research.

Rationale for a Computer Search

We have discussed a variety of bibliographic tools for the identification of psychological literature. These include research literature published in books and journals over a range of disciplines: psychology, sociology, management, education, and medicine. Searching the many tools relevant to a particular topic can be time-consuming, especially if the topic is related to two or more fields and if use of two or more indexes is necessary. A search may be particularly difficult if it involves a topic combining two, three, or more concepts. In the case of recent research topics or those employing new terminology, the controlled vocabulary used in some indexes may not accurately reflect the exact concept that you seek. If you are faced with such a complex multifaceted search, your task will be eased by the use of a computer.

Many indexes and abstracting services have been produced by computers. Beginning in the late 1960s, publishers began making the computer records from which their print indexes are produced available for searching via computer terminals. This service, commonly called *online bibliographic searching,* allows the researcher to bypass the cumbersome task of manually searching printed indexes. This is especially important when your topic combines two or more concepts or is not adequately represented by subject headings used in print indexes. The result of a computer search is a list of citations to literature that is tailored to your particular research topic.

Until recently, computer searches were performed only by librarians experienced in the use of computer databases. In recent years, companies that provide access to online databases to libraries have begun to offer the same services directly to researchers who have their own terminals, a modem allowing them to access a computer using telephone lines, and a subscriber password. These "user-friendly" systems allow individuals to perform their own searches, receive results at their terminal, and be billed directly for the cost of a search. Because these services are most beneficial to those who need frequent literature searches in many databases, faculty and researchers are more likely to benefit from them than students.

Advances in information storage, and specifically compact-disc technology, provide a third alternative. *Compact disc–read only memory* (commonly known as *CD-ROM*) allows libraries to supplant several years of printed indexes and abstracts with one 5-inch computer disc. Using a special disc reader, a microcomputer, and appropriate software, many of these CD-ROM indexes are easy to use and allow researchers and students to perform their own computerized searches.

As we discussed in chapter 3, some libraries are supplementing their traditional card catalogs for access to books with computerized catalogs. In some cases, only the most recent books added to the library or only certain types of library materials are in the online catalog. In others, the traditional card catalog has been abandoned altogether in favor of the computerized version.

Unfortunately, not all computerized bibliographic databases, CD-ROM indexes, and library book catalogs use the same approach to finding materials. Taking the example of *Psychological Abstracts,* the commands used to find citations in the online database, *PsycINFO,* are different from those used in the CD-ROM version, *PsycLIT,* both of which differ from those used in any one online book catalog. To confuse things further, some indexes on CD-ROM, such as ERIC, are offered by more than one CD-ROM vendor, each employing different strategies and commands to retrieve the same information. The many varieties of book catalogs present similar problems.

Because of this diversity, you cannot rely on one approach to all computer-readable indexes, abstracts, and book catalogs. The searching techniques used for the computer databases in your library are often explained in brochures and handouts, or you may ask for assistance from a reference librarian. However, we can identify approaches to computer searching that are reasonably uniform. As with use of the print tools, careful preparation of your search strategy is the key to success. Search results can be improved if you understand what the computer can accomplish. In this chapter we focus on selecting a relevant database from those available, structuring a search strategy, and learning what to expect from a computer search. Finally, in the event that computer searching is not available to you, we discuss other possible sources of computer searches.

Selecting a Database

Table 8–A lists selected databases of possible interest to psychologists. Searches of these databases are frequently available from librarians. Included in the table are information on the name and producer of each database, the subject areas covered by each database, the years for which each database is available (as of late 1991), and the name of the corresponding print index, if one is available. Most are bibliographic databases, meaning that a search of them yields citations to journal articles, books, dissertations, government reports, and other documents.

The databases listed cover various subject areas. Some, such as ERIC (discussed in Chapter 5) and the GPO *Monthly Catalog* (discussed in chapter 7), will be familiar; others, such as Drug Info/ Alcohol Use and Abuse, have no print equivalent. These unpublished indexes can only be searched as computerized databases. Table 8–B contains selected databases in CD-ROM format. For a variety of reasons, many printed and computerized indexes are not available in CD-ROM format. Some, like the ERIC CD-ROM, contain the same citations as those in its print equivalents (*Resources in Education* and *Current Index to Journals in Education*) as well as the ERIC database. But some CD-ROM databases differ from both the printed index and the online database. For example, *PsycLIT* is roughly the equivalent of the *PsycINFO* database. However, like *PsycINFO,* it contains citations to foreign-language journal articles, although it does not include citations to doctoral dissertations. In 1992, the complete 4-year publication coverage of *PsycBOOKS* will be incorporated into PsycLIT, and ongoing coverage of chapters and books will continue with PsycLIT updates. As mentioned in chapter 4, *Psychological Abstracts* contains citations to neither foreign-language journal articles nor to doctoral dissertations. Therefore, it

TABLE 8–A Selected Databases in Psychology

Database	Producer	Subject Areas	Dates Available	Print Equivalents
		Behavioral Sciences		
ABI/INFORM	UMI/Data Courier, Inc.	Business and management	1971+	None
Child Abuse and Neglect	National Center on Child Abuse and Neglect	Child abuse	1965+	No exact equivalent
DRUGINFO/Alcohol Use and Abuse	Drug Information Services, University of Minnesota	Psychological and socio-logical aspects of drug and alcohol abuse	1968+	None
ERIC	Educational Resources Information Center	Education	1966+	*Research/Resources in Education, Current Index to Journals in Education*
Educational Testing Service Test Collection	Educational Testing Service	Educational, psychological, and occupational measurement instruments	current and restrospective	No exact equivalent
Family Resources Database	National Council on Family Relations	Marriage and the family	1970+	*Inventory of Marriage and Family Literature*
Health and Psychosocial Instruments	Behavioral Measurement Database Services, University of Pittsburgh	Testing instruments	1985+	None
Linguistics and Language Behavior Abstracts	Sociological Abstracts, Inc.	Linguistics and language	1973+	*Linguistics and Language Behavior Abstracts*
Management Contents	Information Access Co.	Business and management	1974+	*Management Contents*
Mental Health Abstracts	IFI/Plenum Data Co.	Mental health	1969+	No exact equivalent
Mental Measurements Yearbook	Buros Institute of Mental Measurements, University of Nebraska	Published testing instruments	1972+	*Mental Measurements Yearbook*, minus reference lists
PsycINFO	American Psychological Association	Psychology	1967+	*Psychological Abstracts* plus 25% more citations after 1980
REHABDATA	National Rehabilitation Information Center	Rehabilitation of the physically or mentally disabled	1956+	None

Behavioral Sciences				
Social SCISEARCH	Institute for Scientific Information	Social sciences	1972+	*Social Sciences Citation Index*
Sociological Abstracts	Sociological Abstracts, Inc.	Sociology	1963+	*Sociological Abstracts*
Sciences				
BIOSIS Previews	BIOSIS, Inc.	Biology and life sciences	1969+	*Biological Abstracts, Biological Abstracts/RRM*
MEDLINE	National Library of Medicine	Biomedicine	1966+	*Index Medicus, Index to Dental Literature, International Nursing Index*
SCISEARCH	Institute for Scientific Information	Sciences	1974+	*Science Citation Index*
Multidisciplinary				
Dissertation Abstracts Online	University Microfilms International	Doctoral dissertations and masters theses reproduced by UMI	1861+	*Dissertation Abstracts International, American Doctoral Dissertations, Comprehensive Dissertations Index, Masters Abstracts International*
EPIC	Online Computer Library Center, Inc.	Books, journal titles, audiovisual materials, and other formats	No limit by year	None
GPO Monthly Catalog	Government Printing Office	Unclassified government documents	1976+	*Monthly Catalog of United States Government Publications*

TABLE 8–B

Selected Databases in CD-ROM Format

Database	Dates Available
ABI/Inform	1971+
Biological Abstracts	1990+
Dissertation Abstracts International	1861+
ERIC	1966+
GPO Monthly Catalog	1976+
MEDLINE	1966+
NTIS	1983+
PsycLIT	1974+
Sociofile	1974+
Social Sciences Citation Index	1981+

is important to consult whatever instructional materials your library provides to determine what a CD-ROM database includes. Many CD-ROM databases also include "help" screens that provide this and more information, as well as tutorials that guide you through the basic search process.

The number and types of databases change frequently. New databases are made available, while others are discontinued or change their scope. This is particularly true of CD-ROM technology, because the application of this technology to indexes and abstracts is relatively new. For more recent information, consult a current directory of databases, such as *Computer-Readable Databases.*

Chapter Example: Eating Disorder Tendencies Among Male Athletes

In this chapter, we will focus on eating disorders. Although there are three common forms of eating disorder—anorexia, bulimia, and obesity—we limit our attention to anorexia and bulimia. These are complex problems with psychological, sociological, and physical components.

There are a number of similarities between anorexia and bulimia. For both anorexics and bulimics, there is an extreme fear of being fat. Sufferers have a distorted sense of body image. They typically have been involved in weight-loss programs and view themselves as fat regardless of their actual weight, even if they have become emaciated. Both conditions have been most commonly reported among young, Caucasian women, from the middle and upper classes in developed countries. Both are difficult to treat and may be fatal if not treated effectively. (American Medical Association [AMA], 1989; Beaumont, 1988; Hsu, 1990). Differences between the two disorders are sufficiently significant, however, that sources such as Brownell and Foreyt (1986) choose to deal with them independently.

In anorexia, the individual has an aversion to food and refuses to eat. The condition usually begins with normal dieting activity. However, the anorexic is unwilling to eat normally after significant weight loss (i.e., 15% or more of original weight). Additional symptoms and complications of anorexia may include amenorrhea, overactivity, hypotension, bradycardia, dehydration, anemia, and intolerance to cold (AMA, 1989; Beaumont, 1988; Hsu, 1990; Mitchell, 1986a).

Bulimia is marked by an abnormal craving for food along with successive cycles of binge eating followed by purging through self-induced vomiting or laxative use. Bulimics often have a history of anorexia and high standards of bodily thinness. The bulimic is typically secretive about binge eating and purging episodes. Additional symptoms and complications of bulimia include low self-esteem, chronic anxiety, depression, guilt following a binge, repeated attempts to lose weight with very restrictive diets, frequent weight fluctuations (>10 pounds), and damage to teeth from stomach acid (AMA, 1989; Heatherton & Baumeister, 1991; Hsu, 1990; Mitchell, 1986b).

Different treatment approaches to anorexia and bulimia have shown varying degrees of success. Depending on the severity of the problem, successful treatment programs may require an intense, multidisciplinary, multipronged approach. Treatment of severe cases may involve psychotherapy and family therapy to modify the patient's view of eating, body image, and related psychological components; hospitalization to restore weight loss in severely underweight patients, allowing monitoring of eating behaviors; behavior therapy to reinforce appropriate eating behaviors; pharmacotherapy in the event of problems such as severe depression; and medical treatment for significant physical complications. Relapses from both anorexia and bulimia are common (Hsu, 1990).

Most eating disorder research has focused on women, although some men also are affected. Men active in some sports in which weight is an important component might be disposed to eating disorders; for example, wrestlers, weightlifters, and jockeys all must attain or maintain a specific weight range. Therefore, our search focuses on whether male athletes share a propensity to the behavioral components of eating disorders.

Constructing the Search Strategy

Selecting search terms is essentially the same whether you conduct a manual or a computer search. You must identify key words, terms, and authors of relevant research (see chapters 2, 3, and 4). You should consult a thesaurus, if available, in this process (see chapters 3, 4, and 5).

We have selected the *PsycLIT* database on CD-ROM, which is roughly the equivalent of *Psychological Abstracts* from 1974 to the present and which uses the *Thesaurus of Psychological Index Terms* as its source of controlled vocabulary (see chapter 4 for details). As mentioned earlier in the chapter, *PsycLIT* includes citations to foreign-language journal articles that no longer appear in the print indexes. (Beginning in 1992, *PsycLIT* includes chapter and book citations. Coverage begins with 1987 publications initially included in *PsycBOOKS.*)

Our sample topic contains three separate concepts: eating disorders, athletes, and men (as a specific subject population). Each concept represents one set of descriptors and citations: citations on eating disorders, citations on athletes, and citations on men. If we searched the print indexes, we would find a few relevant references listed under each of these topics. We would, however, also find a much larger number of irrelevant sources. For example, using the subject term eating disorders, we would identify many sources; but a large proportion would deal with populations other than that of human males. Additionally, most probably would not be concerned with athletes. Only citations that deal with all three concepts are relevant to this topic. The search process should thus be a subset composed by the intersection (symbolized ∩) of these three larger sets. The Venn diagram in Figure 8–A contains a pictorial representation of this logical structure.

Once you have outlined the general structure of a search, you must identify specific search terms for each concept. Using the Relationship Section of the *Thesaurus,* we find that the descriptor used for the concept of *eating disorders* is *appetite disorders.* Among the narrower terms listed are *anorexia nervosa* and *bulimia,* both of which are relevant to our topic. The *Thesaurus* includes the subject heading *athletes,* which directly corresponds to that concept in our search. Under *men,* there is a cross-reference to the acceptable descriptor, *human males.* This subject heading has several narrower terms, but none are relevant to our topic.

An advantage of most computer searches is that they are not limited to the controlled vocabulary of a thesaurus. Through *free-text*

FIGURE 8–A

A Venn diagram showing intersection (∩) of three sets of concepts to yield a subset of highly relevant documents

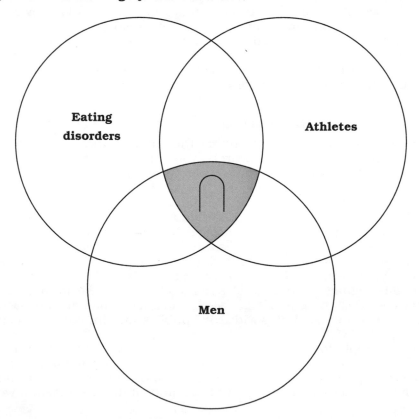

Eating disorders

Athletes

Men

searching (searching words and phrases as they appear in the text of an abstract, a title, and so forth), relevant terms that may not appear in a thesaurus can be searched. Thus we can incorporate synonyms in our list of search terms that are not otherwise represented in the *Thesaurus*. For example, it allows us to add the phrase *eating disorders*, which appears frequently in the research literature, to supplement the *Thesaurus* descriptors *appetite disorders*, *anorexia nervosa*, and *bulimia*. In addition, *bulimia* was not included in the controlled vocabulary until 1985, although *PsycLIT* contains citations from 1974. Therefore, we could include it both as a descriptor and a free-text search term. For the *athletes* concept, we might consider adding the broader *Thesaurus* term *sports* and the related subject heading *athletic participation*. In addition to the *Thesaurus* term *human males*, we can add our free-text term *men*. Because our topic deals with athletes and sports, and therefore the results will contain only references dealing with humans, we can also add *males* or *male* to our list of subject terms.

Table 8–C presents revised and enlarged sets of search terms for the topic we selected. In a search, you would typically instruct the computer first to collect citations indexed under each concept (e.g., all citations on appetite disorders and its related terms). Then you would instruct the computer to combine the three sets, identifying only those citations that contain at least one descriptor or term from each of the three concept groups. The result is a subset of relevant bibliographic citations.

You can further restrict a computer search in several ways. You can exclude documents published in a language that you cannot read. You can limit citations to studies using only human or animal subjects. Of human studies, you can limit the results to those studying a specific age group. Perhaps you would like to limit the search to publications within a particular period of time, such as the last five years. In the case of a search using the *PsycINFO* database, you might want to exclude particular types of publications, such as dissertations, which many libraries do not purchase.

As we discussed earlier in this chapter, there are a large number of databases and database producers, as well as a variety of database vendors. This diversity can be confusing, especially if you must search more than one database or CD-ROM product. For example, the truncation feature available on most systems, the ability

TABLE 8–C

Computer-Search Terms From Three Concept Sets

Concept	Computer Search Terms	
Eating disorders	Appetite disorders[b]	Anorexia nervosa[b]
	Bulimia[ab]	
	Eating disorders[a]	
Athletes	Athletes[b]	Sports[b]
	Athletic participation[b]	
Men	Human males[b]	Men[a]
		Male(s)[a]

[a]Non-*Thesaurus*, free-text terms
[b]Terms used as descriptors in the *Thesaurus*.

to search for terms beginning with a specific root word, can be expressed by different characters depending on the system used: "male*", "male?", or "male$". Fortunately, most database producers and vendors provide helpful guides to the use of their products. These take the form of brochures and workbooks, menus or "help" screens, quick reference cards, disk tutorials, and so forth. As in the case of formulating a list of search terms and consulting a relevant thesaurus, using the available search aids before beginning your search will translate into better results.

A Few Caveats

A computer search can save you a considerable amount of time over conducting the same literature search in print indexes. However, if you do not use some caution, a computer can actually lengthen your literature search process.

The ease with which a list of citations can be generated prompts many students to formulate their search too broadly, resulting in lists of hundreds of citations. Their reasoning is that irrelevant citations can be crossed off their list and discarded later. However, in order to do so, you will have to read many titles and abstracts to discard the irrelevant ones, thus defeating your goal of saving time. It is better to start with a narrow, well-defined search, then broaden the concepts and terms you use if your search results in too few citations.

A second caveat concerns the basic limitations of most computer systems and illustrates the need for a well-considered search strategy. The computer cannot interpret shades of meaning that are inherent in language, and therefore will produce citations based on the commands given, whether or not the question you ask reflects what you want. For example, your search strategy might include the *Thesaurus* descriptor *Aged,* a synonym for elderly. However, if this were used as a free-text term, the computer will find all occurrences of this word, regardless of its context. Therefore, you might retrieve an article including the phrase "infants aged two through four" in the abstract.

Typographical errors can result in a similar problem. Using our example above, the *Thesaurus* term entered as *athlete* will not yield the same citations as the correct term, *athletes.* In addition, technical terms should be entered with particular care. If your search results in no references for a term, that may indicate a spelling or typing error.

Most publishers began producing indexes from computer databases in the late 1960s or early 1970s, and few publishers have included citations from earlier years. Only two databases listed in Table 8–A contain citations from earlier than 1960, and many CD-ROM computer files concentrate on the most recent years. For this reason, you cannot rely on computer databases for retrospective literature searches. Using print indexes and abstracts is essential to supplement a computer search for complete coverage of a topic.

Search Results

Figure 8–B presents a *Psychological Abstracts* citation with its equivalent *PsycLIT* computer-generated citation. (Please note: The

FIGURE 8-B

Entry from *Psychological Abstracts* (Vol. 75, issue 6, 1988, p. 1530), with the corresponding subject-access entry from the annual *Subject Index* (Vol. 75, 1988, p. 197), and the corresponding citation as it appears in the *PsycLIT* database.

75: 16870–16882   *PERSONALITY*   ③ₐ

⑪ₐ   16879. **King, Michael B. & Mezey, Gillian.** (U London, Inst of Psychiatry, England) **Eating behaviour of male racing jockeys.**   ①ₐ

②ₐ   *Psychological Medicine*, 1987(Feb), Vol 17(1), 249–253. —Screened 14 male jockeys (aged 19–35 yrs) based in racing stables in England, using a 26-item eating attitudes test (EAT). The mean score of the EAT was 14.9, significantly above that reported for males in other studies. 10 jockeys agreed to a full psychiatric and eating interview.

④ₐ   The majority of jockeys interviewed reported food avoidance, the use of saunas, and the abuse of laxatives. Diuretics and appetite suppressants were also used. Bingeing was common, but self-induced vomiting was unusual. Current weights were 13% below and the lowest reported weights were 21% below matched population mean weights. The relationship between these forms of eating behavior and clinical eating disorders is discussed.   ⑤ₐ

---

⑥ₐ   **SUBJECT INDEX**

Athletes
   attitudes toward eating & weight control, 19–35 yr old male
      jockeys, England, implications for eating disorders, 16879

```
TI: Eating behaviour of male racing jockeys.
AU: King,-Michael-B.; Mezey,-Gillian
IN: U London, Inst of Psychiatry, England
JN: Psychological-Medicine; 1987 Feb Vol 17(1) 249-253
LA: English
PY: 1987
AB:  Screened 14 male jockeys (aged 19-35 yrs) based in racing stables in
England, using a 26-item eating attitudes test (EAT). The mean score of the EAT
was 14.9, significantly above that reported for males in other studies. 10
jockeys agreed to a full psychiatric and eating interview. The majority of
jockeys interviewed reported food avoidance, the use of saunas, and the abuse
of laxatives. Diuretics and appetite suppressants were also used. Bingeing was
common, but self-induced vomiting was unusual. Current weights were 13% below
and the lowest reported weights were 21% below matched population mean
weights. The relationship between these forms of eating behavior and clinical
eating disorders is discussed. (PsycLIT Database Copyright 1988 American
Psychological Assn, all rights reserved)
KP:  attitudes toward eating & weight control; 19-35 yr old male jockeys;
England; implications for eating disorders
DE:  EATING-; ATHLETES-; WEIGHT-CONTROL; HUMAN-MALES; ADULT-ATTITUDES;
ADULTHOOD-
PO: Human
AG: Adult
AN: 75-16879
```

format of the computer-generated citation may vary slightly depending on the search service and database used.) Much of the information provided by the two citations is identical: the title (**1,1a**), the names of the authors (**2,2a**), the institutional affiliation (**3,3a**), the bibliographic information (**4,4a**), and the abstract (**5,5a**).

The computer-generated citation contains considerable information that is not included in the *PA* print version. Appended to the computer citation (**6**) is the brief descriptive phrase that identifies this article in the subject index (**6a**). The computer citation may also contain the language of publication (**7**), the year of publication (**8**), whether the population studied was human or animal (**9**), and, in the case of human populations, the age group studied (**10**). The abstract number in the computer-generated citation (**11**) includes the number of the *PA* volume in which this citation appears (**11a**).

The PsycLIT citation also includes the list of *Thesaurus* descriptors used to index this article (**12**). You can use this list of terms to expand and refine your list of search terms in the same way that you used catalog tracings in chapter 3. Another valuable approach is to select a key journal article, find the article by searching by author or title in *PsycLIT*, and use the list of relevant *Thesaurus* descriptors assigned to index that article to modify your search strategy.

Sources of Computer-Search Services

Many college and university libraries offer online bibliographic searching as a service of their reference or public-service department. Some libraries make this service available to all members of the academic community, whereas others may restrict it to faculty members. Some libraries do not charge for the service, others charge a minimal fee (from $3 to $10 per search), and others expect the requester to bear the full cost of the computer search (often $25 or more). A librarian or a pamphlet on the services offered by your library can inform you of the availability of these services on your campus.

If this service is not available in your library, a reference librarian can provide advice on obtaining a computer search. You may be able to obtain assistance from another library in your geographic region. If you are willing to pay for a computer search, you may wish to investigate a professional service. One such service is PASAR, available from *PsycINFO* at the American Psychological Association. Searches of the *PsycINFO* database are performed on a full cost-recovery basis. Searches are also available through companies that provide information commercially and have access to a broad range of databases. Before placing a search request, it is wise to obtain an estimate of the cost. For a list of companies offering such services, consult a directory such as *North American Online Directory*.

References

American Medical Association. (1989). *American Medical Association home medical encyclopedia.* New York: Random House.

Beaumont, P. J. V. (1988). Recent advances concerning eating disorders. *Current Opinion in Psychiatry, 1,* 155–164.

Brownell, K. D., & Foreyt, J. P. (Eds.). (1986). *Handbook of eating disorders.* New York: Basic Books.

Heatherton, T. F., & Baumeister, R. F. (1991). Binge eating as escape from self-awareness. *Psychological Bulletin, 110,* 86–108.

IIsu, L. K. G. (1990). *Eating disorders.* New York: Guilford Press.

Mitchell, J. E. (1986a). Anorexia nervosa: Medical and physiological aspects. In K. D. Brownell & J. P. Foreyt (Eds.). *Handbook of eating disorders* (pp. 247–265). New York: Basic Books.

Mitchell, J. E. (1986b). Bulimia: Medical and physiological aspects. In K. D. Brownell & J. P. Foreyt (Eds.). *Handbook of eating disorders* (pp. 379–386). New York: Basic Books.

9 Psychological Tests and Measures

Sources Discussed

Mental Measurements Yearbook

> Buros, O. K. (Ed.). *Mental measurements yearbook.* Highland Park, NJ: Gryphon Press. (1938). *1938 Mental measurements yearbook.* (1978). *Eighth mental measurements yearbook.*

> Mitchell, J. V., Jr. (Ed.). (1985). *Ninth mental measurements yearbook* (Vols. 1–2). Lincoln, NE: Buros Institute of Mental Measurements, University of Nebraska.

> Conoley, J. C., & Kramer, J. J. (Eds.). (1989–present). *Tenth mental measurements yearbook.* Lincoln, NE: Buros Institute of Mental Measurements, University of Nebraska. Biennial.

Tests in Print

> Buros, O. K. (Ed.). (1961). *Tests in print.* Highland Park, NJ: Gryphon Press.

> Buros, O. K. (Ed.). (1974). *Tests in print II.* Highland Park, NJ: Gryphon Press.

> Mitchell, J. V. (Ed.). (1983). *Tests in print III.* Lincoln, NE: Buros Institute of Mental Measurements, University of Nebraska.

Directory of Unpublished Experimental Mental Measures

> Goldman, B. A., & Saunders, J. L. (Eds.). (1974). *Directory of unpublished experimental mental measures* (Vol. 1). New York: Behavioral Publications.

> Goldman, B. A., & Busch, J. C. (Eds.). (1978, 1982). *Directory of unpublished experimental mental measures* (Vols. 2–3). New York: Human Sciences Press.

> Goldman, B. A., and Osborne, W. L. (1985). *Directory of unpublished experimental mental measures* (Vol. 4). Human Sciences Press.

> Goldman, B., & Mitchell, D. (1990). *Directory of unpublished experimental mental measures* (Vol. 5). Dubuque, IA: William C. Brown.

Educational Testing Service. (1986–present). *The ETS Test Collection Catalog.* Phoenix, AZ: Oryx.

Keyser, D. J., & Sweetland, R. C. (Eds.). (1984–present). *Test critiques.* Kansas City, MO: Test Corporation of America.

Sweetland, R. C., & Keyser, D. J. (Eds.). (1990). *Tests* (3rd ed.). Austin, TX: PRO-ED.

Need for Information on Tests

There are many situations in which a psychologist may need information about a psychological test. For example, school psychologists evaluate children referred by classroom teachers who suspect learning disabilities. The school psychologist must know which of the many tests available are most appropriate to ascertain whether a learning disability exists and, if so, its nature and severity. A vocational counselor uses tests to gather information about interests, aptitudes, and skills to advise people regarding career options. He or she must know which tests are best for which kinds of career counseling situations. A researcher may use tests to measure attitudes, behaviors, abilities, or other variables relevant to a particular research hypothesis. The researcher might construct a new measuring instrument or use one that already exists. A new measure may lack reliability or validity and may not allow comparison with prior research. Thus the researcher will want to know about existing tests and measures appropriate to the particular research situation.

There exist various situations in which you, as a student, may need information about psychological tests. You may be enrolled in a course in tests and measurements in which you are required to investigate a variety of psychological tests. You may be designing a research project and need to select or devise a relevant test or other measuring instrument. You may be writing a paper on a topic that relies heavily on research involving the use of one or several particular tests or measures. As such, you may need to understand thoroughly the assumptions, theoretical and empirical structure, and mechanics of the measures used in that research.

Psychological tests or measures of one type or another are used in most research in psychology. Tests and measures represent particular ways of observing and gathering information about psychological concepts. A psychological concept, such as personality, may be operationally defined in many ways.

Different operational definitions of the same psychological concept may lead to different measurement strategies. For example, a researcher has many options when deciding how to measure personality. Two very different strategies for the measurement of personality might involve the use of a structured, objective personality inventory such as the Minnesota Multiphasic Personality Inventory (Hathaway & McKinley, 1970) or of a less structured, projective personality test such as the Rorschach Inkblot Test (Rorschach, 1942). These two tests were developed in different ways, they involve radically different measurement strategies, and they yield different kinds of information about personality. As a result, the selection of one test may lead to research findings that are at odds with the findings resulting from another test selection. For this reason, the decision to use a particular test in the design of a study will have a critical impact on the findings that emerge from the research. As a researcher, you must be aware of the influence of differing measurement strategies on the research that you conduct. As a reader of the research of others, you must be aware of these same issues in order to understand and compare intelligently the findings of studies employing dissimilar measurement strategies. To develop this awareness, you must locate information on the test(s) under consideration.

Thousands of tests have been created. For purposes of locating them, they may be grouped in two general classes: published tests and unpublished tests. Published tests may be purchased by psychologists from commercial test publishers, such as the Consulting Psychologists Press, the Educational Testing Service, and the Psychological Corporation. Many published tests are heavily used and are therefore readily available. In contrast, unpublished tests and measures are not available from commercial publishers. They may be less well known to psychologists and used less frequently by them. The primary application of unpublished tests is in research, and such tests may be mentioned or described in only one or a few research reports.

In this chapter, we discuss sources of information about psychological tests and measures. We focus attention first on published tests and then on unpublished tests.

Chapter Example: Personality Research Form

To illustrate the use of testing sources, we focus on personality assessment. There are many types of psychological tests and measures in the field of personality. Psychological tests may be developed in a variety of ways. Anastasi (1988) identified at least four different approaches to the development of personality measures: (a) content validation (e.g., Mooney Problem Checklist), (b) empirical criterion keying (e.g., Minnesota Multiphasic Personality Inventory), (c) factor analysis (e.g., Sixteen Personality Factor Questionnaire), and (d) psychological theory (e.g., Myers-Briggs Type Indicator).

For illustrative purposes, we selected a published psychological measure that is widely used, objective, scorable and interpretable by psychology students, and recently developed or revised. Furthermore, we wished to inspect a measure that is interpretable within the context of a personality theory. A number of personality measures were reviewed and eliminated because they did not meet these criteria. For example, the Thematic Apperception Test (Murray, 1971) is a projective test that requires much training to use. The Edwards Personal Preference Schedule (Edwards, 1959) has not been revised recently. Continuing through Anastasi (1988), the section on personality includes a chapter on self-report personality inventories, including the Personality Research Form. The third edition of the Personality Research Form (PRF) was published in 1987. The PRF was developed by Douglas N. Jackson (1984) for use in research to measure personality traits of normal individuals; it is not intended as a measure of psychopathology. It is an objective personality test, with scales derived from the need theory of Henry Murray (1938). The PRF assesses that part of Murray's theory concerning psychological needs (traits). Depending on the form used, it reports either 14 or 20 dimensions. Scales are provided for several personality dimensions (e.g., achievement, affiliation, dominance, nurturance, and play). Checking the manual (Jackson, 1984), the

PRF appears to have been carefully constructed and statistically well designed, and to have good internal consistency and reliability characteristics.

The PRF does, however, appear to have some limitations. It does not assess Murray's (1938) notion of presses. Nor does it deal with issues such as the relationship between needs and presses, interaction among needs, development of personality, or relationship between personality and behavior. It is insensitive to the more contemporary influences of social learning theory and behavioral psychology on personality assessment noted by Lanyon (1984).

We need to learn more about the strengths and weaknesses of the PRF.

Published Tests

The most extensive coverage of published standardized tests commercially available in the English-speaking world is provided by the *Mental Measurements Yearbooks (MMY)* and their companion publications. The first eight *MMY* volumes, published from 1938 through 1978, were edited by Oscar Krisen Buros, with the assistance of Luella Buros. Hence, they are still widely referred to simply as "Buros." Contrary to the title, *MMY* volumes are not published every year. Until the ninth edition, they appeared at 6- to 10-year intervals. Beginning in 1988, new editions are being published every other year, with a paper supplement appearing in intervening years.

The *MMY* volumes provide detailed factual information on published tests for use with English-speaking subjects and critical reviews of most of those tests. Additionally, volumes provide extensive bibliographies of references to tests listed in *MMY* and, in older editions, lists and reviews of books on testing and measurement. The *MMY* editions supplement each other, with succeeding editions including only new tests, substantially revised tests, and new information about previously reviewed tests.

A related source begun by O. K. Buros is *Tests in Print (TIP)*, published in 1961. This was followed in 1974 by *Tests in Print II (TIP2)* and in 1983 by *Tests in Print III (TIP3)*. The purpose of these volumes is to supplement material included in the *MMY* volumes by providing purchasing information for tests and information on tests that are out of print and no longer available for purchase from commercial publishers. *TIP3* contains 2,672 test entries, with indexes by title, a classified subject arrangement, publisher, and name. *TIP3* also acts as a comprehensive index to in-print tests in the first eight *MMY*s, as well as to those tests that have gone out-of-print since they were cited in *TIP2* or the *Eighth MMY*.

The *Tenth MMY* contains information on 396 new or revised tests issued after publication of the *Ninth MMY* in 1985 and incorporates the reviews published in the ninth edition's supplement in 1988. It also provides reviews for tests that had appeared in the previous *MMY* but which had not received reviews. A total of 569 original reviews by 303 contributors accompany 351 test entries, so that almost 90% of the tests included receive a critical review, with 60% of the tests receiving more than one review (Conoley and Kramer, 1989).

In addition to the 10 *MMY*s and 3 *TIP*s, Buros and his successors produced numerous monographs containing information in particular areas. These monographs are intended for the psychologist who does not need the complete coverage of all topics provided by *MMY*. They are similar in form and content to *MMY* and cover the areas of personality, reading, intelligence, and so forth. Because they are no longer published and so many of the tests included in these volumes have since been revised, they are used primarily for retrospective coverage of tests.

Using the *Mental Measurements Yearbook*

Because we already know the name of the test we seek (Personality Research Form, third edition), we turn immediately to the Tests and Reviews section of the *Tenth MMY*, in which tests are listed alphabetically by their titles. Here we find that the PRF is test number 282. In addition to the basic title arrangement, the *MMY* contains six indexes: Index of Titles, Index of Acronyms, Classified Subject Index, Publishers Directory and Index, Index of Names, and Score Index. The Index of Titles is useful for tests that change titles over one or more editions or that are commonly known or referred to in professional literature by alternate titles. Because the Personality Research Form is often known by its acryonym (PRF), we would be able to locate it by using the Index of Acronyms. The test is also listed alphabetically under the name of its author, Douglas N. Jackson, in the Index of Names.

The Classified Subject Index lists each test and the population for which it is intended under 16 broad categories: achievement, intelligence and scholastic aptitude, sensory-motor, vocations, and so forth. In this case, the Personality Research Form is listed under the category of Personality. Had we not known about the PRF, we could have consulted the Classified Subject Index and found information about numerous personality tests. By using the Score Index, we can locate tests that measure specific variables or are intended to measure a particular aspect (e.g., affiliation, autonomy, or nurturance). Finally, the Publishers Directory and Index lists test numbers by their publishers and includes publishers' addresses. All indexes provide a test number (not the page number) by which tests are listed sequentially in the body of the *MMY*.

For information about the Personality Research Form, we turn to test entry 282 in the Tests and Reviews section of the *Tenth MMY*. Every test entry follows the same general format, illustrated in Figure 9–A for the PRF. Each test description begins with the test entry number (**1**). The test title (**2**) appears in boldface print, followed by a general statement about the purpose of the test (**3**), in this case quoted from the test's manual. It also provides information on the groups for which the test is intended (**4**), the publication dates for forms incorporating the test and support documentation (**5**), the acronym by which the test is often referred (**6**), and brief factual notes about the test (**7**). (In this case, the description notes that a previous edition of the test, which is still available for purchase, was included in the ninth edition of the *MMY* as test number 950). This test has six forms or versions (**8**). Cost information for the forms and supporting documentation (**9**), the name of the author (**10**),

▰▰▰ FIGURE 9–A

Excerpts from a review of the Personality Research Form, third edition, from J. C. Conoley and J. J. Kramer (Eds.), *Tenth Mental Measurements Yearbook* (1989, pp 630–632).

[282] Personality Research Form, 3rd Edition

[282]

Personality Research Form, 3rd Edition.
Purpose: Yields "a set of scores for personality traits broadly relevant to the functioning of individuals in a wide variety of situations." Grade 6–college, adults; 1965–87; PRF; previous edition (9:950) still available; 6 forms; 1987 price data: $19 per 25 reusable test booklets (specify form); $5 per scoring template (specify Form E, A/B, or AA/BB); $4.75 per 25 answer sheets; $4.75 per 25 profiles (specify Form E, A/B, or AA/BB); $8 per manual ('84, 72 pages); $27.50 per examination kit including 10 reusable booklets, manual, scoring template, 25 answer sheets, and 25 profiles (specify form); Douglas N. Jackson; Research Psychologists Press, Inc.*

a) FORM A. Age 16–Adult; 1965–85; 15 scores: Achievement, Affiliation, Aggression, Autonomy, Dominance, Endurance, Exhibition, Harmavoidance, Impulsivity, Nurturance, Order, Play, Social Recognition, Understanding, Infrequency; (30–45) minutes.

• • •

See 9:950 (42 references); see also T3:1798 (116 references); for a review by Robert Hogan of an earlier edition, see 8:643 (132 references); see also T3:1322 (23 references); for reviews by Anne Anastasi, E. Lowell Kelly, and Jerry Wiggins, and

• • •

TEST REFERENCES

1. Williams R. L., Gutsch, K. U., Kazelskis, R., Verstegen, J. P., & Scanlon, J. (1980). An investigation of relationships between level of alcohol use impairment and personality characteristics. *Addictive Behavior,* 5, 107–112.
2. Gaddy, C. D., Glass, C. R., & Arnkoff, D. B. (1983). Career involvement of women in dual-career families: The influence of sex role identity. *Journal of Counseling Psychology,* 30, 388-394.
3. Banks, S., Mooney, W. T., Mucowski, R. J., & Williams, R. (1984). Progress in the evaluation and prediction of successful candidates for religious careers. *Counseling and Values,* 28, 82-91.

• • •

Review of the Personality Research Form, 3rd Edition by ROBERT HOGAN, McFarlin Professor of Psychology, University of Tulsa, Tulsa, OK:
Tests can be evaluated in terms of four general questions. The first concerns what the test measures and why; this asks about the conceptual foundations of the test. The Personality Research Form (PRF) is designed to assess, depending on the form, 15 to 22 dimensions of normal personality originally defined by Henry Murray (1938) in his *Explorations in Personality.* These dimensions appear on other standardized inventories as well as the PRF, so the choice is well precedented. Nonetheless, these variables were chosen primarily, one senses, because they were there, and because they have name recognition value in the personality research community.

• • •

and the publisher (**11**) follow. The asterisk (**12**) at the end of this description indicates that the information was compiled after an examinatiom of the actual test materials.

Because the PRF consists of several distinct forms for use with different populations or intended to measure specific traits, this entry contains detailed information for each form. For example, the description of Form A (**13**) parallels information provided for the test as a whole: It is intended for use with adults ages 16 and up and has been published in several versions in the years indicated. In addition, the description tells us the subscales for which test scores are available (**14**) and the administration time required (**15**).

Often, there will be references to reviews and reference lists appearing in other Buros series for this test or previous versions of the test. For example, the previous edition of the test was cited in the *Ninth MMY*, test number 950, and it provided 42 references (**16**). The test was also included in *TIP3*, test number 1798, with 116 references (**17**). There are numerous references to *TIP* volumes and previous *MMY* volumes, including several critical reviews of earlier editions. Following these cross-references is a list of references (**18**) to materials concerning the development, evaluation, and use of the test. Next is a critical review of the test (**19**), which begins with the name and position of the reviewer.

Other Information Sources for Published Tests

Until the mid-1980s, the Buros series stood alone in providing comprehensive access to and authoritative reviews of published tests. Because of the long publishing history of the Buros volumes, it remains the prominent source for researchers. A second, more recent publication that reviews published tests is *Test Critiques*. First published in 1984, volumes appear at the rate of one per year, each volume containing approximately 100 test reviews. Tests and their reviews are arranged by test title. Each volume contains several indexes: Index of Test Titles, Index of Test Publishers, Index of Test Authors/Reviewers, and Subject Index. Beginning with Volume III, the test title, publisher, author, and subject indexes include test entries from the most current and all previous volumes.

Using the Index to Test Titles, we locate an 11-page review of the Personality Research Form in Volume III of *Test Critiques*, illustrated in part in Figure 9–B. Bibliographic information preceding the review is limited to the title (**20**), author (**21**), and publisher information (**22**), and the name and position of the reviewer are provided (**23**). Most reviews in *Test Critiques* follow a fairly standard format, beginning with an introduction and description of the test's intended uses (**24**), followed by technical information, a critique and conclusion, and a list of references. Compared to the *MMY*, *Test Critiques* provides less descriptive information about tests and cites fewer studies in reference lists. However, reviews are usually longer, sometimes employ illustrative charts and tables, and provide more technical data associated with each test. Although many tests will appear in either *MMY* or *Test Critiques*, both should be consulted for complete coverage.

Tests, another source, is a directory of over 3,000 published English-language tests. The measures are categorized under the

FIGURE 9–B

Excerpts from a review of the Personality Research Form, third edition, from D. J. Keyser and R. C. Sweetland (Eds.), *Test Critiques* **(Vol. III, 1985, p. 499).**

(23)

Howard E. A. Tinsley, Ph.D.
Professor of Psychology and Director of Counseling Psychology, Southern Illinois University at Carbondale, Carbondale, Illinois.

(20)

PERSONALITY RESEARCH FORM

(21) *Douglas N. Jackson. Port Huron, Michigan: Research Psychologists Press, Inc.* (22)

Introduction

(24) Development of the Personality Research Form (PRF) was guided by the belief that more rigorous and valid assessment of personality characteristics could be achieved through the application of modern principles of personality and test theory (Jackson, 1984). The goals established for the PRF were to develop an item pool and a set of personality scales relevant to normal human functioning in a wide variety of situations. Jackson (1984) reasoned that if a trait or construct was given a carefully considered, theoretical definition prior to the beginning of scale construction, the need to rely on item analysis of groups of persons identified on the basis of unstable external criteria would be reduced. According to Jackson, the resulting atheoretical grouping of items into scales could thus be avoided, and the instrument would be more broadly relevant to the measurement of normal personality traits. Jackson (1984) recommends the PRF for use in personality research and for measuring normal personality traits in settings such as schools, colleges, clinics, guidance centers, business, and industry. The PRF is not intended to measure psychopathology.

Douglas Jackson, the developer of the PRF, is the author and coauthor of numerous other tests, including the Jackson Personality Inventory (JPI), Jackson Vocational Interest Survey (JVIS), Multidimensional Aptitude Battery (MAB), Career

• • •

areas of psychology, education, and business, with each broad area further subdivided. Although *Tests* does not contain reviews, each measure is accompanied by a brief description, the intended use, cost, and availability. It is designed as a quick guide to finding tests meeting a specific need. It has indexes by publisher, test title, and author, and indexes that allow test selection for use with populations having special testing needs, such as the visually and hearing impaired.

Information Sources for Unpublished Tests

Thousands of tests, questionnaires, and other measuring instruments created by researchers are not commercially available. Often they have been mentioned only briefly in a research report or presented in an article or book. You may find locating such measuring instruments difficult. Information on their technical adequacy (reliability, validity, norms, and so forth) may be scanty, if available at all. Since the 1960s, several sources that attempt to provide access to these various materials have been published.

The *Directory of Unpublished Experimental Mental Measures (Directory)* lists unpublished tests appearing in a large number of psychology and related journals. At present, there are five volumes of the *Directory,* covering tests available in journal articles published in 1970 (Vol. 1), 1971–1972 (Vol. 2), 1973–1974 (Vol. 3), 1974–1980 (Vol. 4), and 1981–1985 (Vol. 5). Included in the *Directory* is a brief description of each measure and a reference to the journal in which information related to the test appeared. Tests are grouped by general type (attitude, personality, and so forth), and a cumulative subject index is included.

Several other sources provide information of possible interest. In *Measures for Psychological Assessment,* Chun, Cobb, and French (1975) compiled 3,000 references to articles in social science journals that reported the use of various tests and measures. *The Sourcebook of Mental Health Measures* (Comrey, Backer, & Glaser, 1973) complements their efforts by listing and abstracting 1,100 tests, questionnaires, rating scales, and inventories not included by Chun, Cobb, and French. *Tests and Measurements in Child Development* (Johnson, 1976; Johnson & Bommarito, 1971), limited to research on children, provides a more focused approach. *Handbook I* (Johnson & Bommarito, 1971) covers tests reported prior to 1965 for infants through children 12 years old. *Handbook II* (Johnson, 1976) expands coverage to infancy through age 18 and includes materials reported from 1966 through 1974. Descriptive information is provided for each measure, accompanied by the source of the information.

Several sources exist in the area of attitude measurement. A three-volume series published by the Survey Research Center at the University of Michigan (Robinson, Athanasiou, & Head, 1969; Robinson, Rusk, & Head, 1968; Robinson, Shaver, & Wrightsman, 1991) covers approximately 300 attitude scales. These volumes provide descriptive information, brief evaluative information, source, and either sample items or the whole measure. M. E. Shaw and J. M. Wright (1967) present approximately 175 attitude measurement scales, including the full test, scoring, and background information.

Together these sources supplement *MMY* by providing information on a wide variety of unpublished measures. Other sources include both published and unpublished measures. The *ETS Test Collection Catalog* includes both unpublished research instruments and commercially available tests and questionnaires owned by the Test Collection of ETS. The catalogs have appeared almost annually, and each includes bibliographic and descriptive information on approximately 1000 tests. Each volume focuses on a specific subject area: Achievement Tests and Measurement Devices, Vocational Tests and Measurement Devices, Tests for Special Populations, Cognitive Aptitude and Intelligence Tests, and Attitude Tests.

An International Directory of Spatial Tests (Eliot & Smith, 1983) includes information on about 400 pencil-and-paper tests that measure spatial ability, such as figural rotations, mazes, and visual memory tests. Published, out-of-print, and unpublished measures are included. *Women and Women's Issues* (Beere, 1979), is a compilation of information on 235 instruments and is, in part, supplemented by 211 instruments included in *Gender Roles: A Handbook of Tests and Measures* (Beere, 1990). They include information about both unpublished and published measures made available through the end of 1977 and mid-1988, respectively.

Using these sources, you can search for information about tests and measures relevant to your research, papers, and courses. One cautionary note, however: Because of the sensitivity of some published psychological tests and measures, you may not find the measures themselves in your college library. Indeed, some libraries, as a matter of policy, do not maintain a collection of psychological tests. Instead, in many cases, you will need to contact a psychologist in a department of psychology, counseling center, or other facility at your college to discuss the availability of a test you wish to examine.

References

Anastasi, A. (1988). *Psychological testing* (6th ed.). New York: Macmillan.

Beere, C. A. (1979). *Women and women's issues: A handbook of tests and measures.* San Francisco: Jossey-Bass.

Beere, C. A. (1990). *Gender roles: A handbook of tests and measures.* New York: Greenwood.

Chun, K., Cobb, S., & French, J. R. P. (1975). *Measures for psychological assessment.* Ann Arbor, MI: Survey Research Center.

Comrey, A. L., Backer, T. E., & Glaser, E. M. (1973). *A sourcebook of mental health measures.* Los Angeles: Prepared for the National Institute of Mental Health by the Human Interaction Research Institute.

Conoley, J. C., & Kramer, J. J. (Eds.). (1989). *Tenth mental measurements yearbook.* Lincoln, NE: Buros Institute of Mental Measurements, University of Nebraska.

Edwards, A. L. (1959). *Edwards Personal Preference Schedule manual.* New York: Psychological Corporation.

Eliot, J., & Smith, I. M. (1983). *An international directory of spatial tests.* Berks, England, NFER-Nelson.

Hathaway, S. R., & McKinley, J. C. (1970). *Booklet for the Minnesota Multiphasic Personality Inventory.* New York: Psychological Corporation.

Jackson, D. N. (1984). *Personality Research Form manual.* Port Huron, MI: Research Psychologists Press.

Johnson, O. G. (Ed.). (1976). *Tests and measuremnets in child development: Handbook II* (2 vols.). San Francisco: Jossey-Bass.

Johnson, O. G., & Bommarito, J. W. (Eds.). (1971). *Tests and measurements in child development: Handbook I.* San Francisco: Jossey-Bass.

Lanyon, R. I. (1984). Personality assessment. *Annual Review of Psychology, 35,* 667–701.

Murray, H. A. (1938). *Explorations in personality.* Cambridge, MA: Harvard University Press.

Murray, H. A. (1971). *Thematic Apperception Test manual.* Cambridge, MA: Harvard University Press.

Robinson, J. P., Athanasiou, R., & Head, K. B. (1969). *Measures of occupational attitudes and occupational characteristics.* Ann Arbor, MI: Survey Research Center.

Robinson, J. P., Rusk, J. G., & Head, K. B. (1968). *Measures of political attitudes.* Ann Arbor, MI: Survey Research Center.

Robinson, J. P., Shaver, P. R., & Wrightsman, L. S. (1991). *Measures of personality and social psychological attitudes.* San Diego, CA: Academic Press.

Rorschach, H. (1942). *Psychodiagnostics: A diagnostic test based on perception* (P. Lemkau & B. Kronenberg, Trans.) Berne, Switzerland: Huber. (1st German ed., 1921: U.S. distributor, Grune & Stratton)

Shaw, M. E., & Wright, J. M. (1967). *Scales for the measurement of attitudes.* New York: McGraw-Hill.

10 Miscellaneous Sources

In previous chapters, we have presented various sources useful for pursuing information on a topic in psychology. The purpose of tools such as *Annual Review of Psychology, Psychological Abstracts,* and *Social Sciences Citation Index* is to construct a retrospective literature review consisting of citations to sources relevant to a topic.

The tools discussed in this chapter serve quite a different purpose. They can broaden your knowledge of a particular area of research. For example, current-awareness tools update a retrospective literature search already undertaken and may identify new directions in research or persons conducting such research. Doctoral dissertations are an important source of unpublished research. Biographical information on a prominent researcher or author may lend his or her thesis support based on information such as academic credentials or current research interests. Book reviews provide informed opinions to help you identify the potential usefulness and reliability of books in the field. Thus the tools presented in this chapter may supplement your knowledge of a given research area.

Chapter Example: Human–Computer Interaction

In this chapter we will focus on the general area of computer-human interaction. This relatively new field draws from disciplines such as cognitive psychology, human factors, industrial engineering, and computer science. In its theoretical form, the focus is on understanding the transactions that take place between people and computerized systems and development of theories and models to understand and predict behavior. The practitioner's approach is to use knowledge of these disciplines in the design of effective user interfaces for systems.

The advent of microprocessors and the use of cathode ray tubes (CRTs) in text editors and home computers, as well as for the control of complex systems (e.g., copiers and printers), has changed much about user interface design. At one time, human-factors engineers and industrial designers were primarily concerned about the location, shape, feel, and so forth of the knobs, dials, levers, switches, labels, and feedback devices they designed for use on hard control panels for equipment. Classic books on human factors (e.g., Kantowitz & Sorkin, 1983; Sanders & McCormick, 1987; Van Cott & Kinkade, 1972) provided important guidance in such tasks. Today's systems are sufficiently large and complex, however, that for many, a hard control would be so large that it could dwarf the machine. Given computer control over increasing numbers of systems elements, many user interfaces have been rendered through CRT-based control panels. Increasingly, the principles of human factors and industrial engineering are being applied to human–computer interaction problems.

Newell and Card (1986) identified some of the critical elements of a psychology of human–computer interaction. Among their points are

- The goal of such study is information that will aid in the design of better systems.
- A psychology of the user is necessary.
- Design decisions are critical in development of effective systems.

Card, Moran, and Newell (1983) argued for a science base of knowledge to support designers with performance-based models.

Norman (1988) believes that we must understand our everyday environment. We must understand people and the tasks they will perform with a system. His study of human error led to the conclusion that

> if an error is possible, someone will make it. The designer must assume that all possible errors will occur and design so as to minimize the chance of the error in the first place, or its effects once it gets made. Errors should be easy to detect, they should have minimal consequences, and if possible, their effects should be reversible. (Norman, 1988, p. 36)

Design uses all of this information to develop an effective user interface. Human–computer user interface designers employ a number of principles in their work such as the following:

- Metaphors used should be consistent with the user's real world experience.

- The user interface should provide a coherent, accurate model of the system. If a model is not provided, the user will develop one, and it may not be correct.
- Feedback about the state of the system and actions the user has taken should be readily available, unambiguous, and clear.
- Design for error. Minimize the opportunity for error. Minimize the consequences of error.
- Provide maps of the environment to enable navigation through a complex interface.

Additional consideration may be found in a variety of sources (e.g., Booth, 1989; Norman, 1983; Shneiderman, 1987; Smith, Irby, Kimball, Verplank, & Harslem, 1982).

A body of literature has appeared describing this field. Both theoretical and applied monographs have been published (e.g., Booth, 1989; Card, Moran, & Newell, 1983; Norman & Draper, 1986; Shneiderman, 1987). New journals have appeared (e.g., *Human–Computer Interaction*) and existing journals (e.g., *International Journal of Man–Machine Studies*) have broadened their focus to cover relevant issues. New conferences have been developed (e.g., CHI Conference on Human Factors in Computer Science). Materials appropriate for the lay public have appeared such as Donald Norman's (1988) *Psychology of Everyday Things*. How can one learn about these things: recent articles, books that have been written, people in the field?

Current-Awareness Services

Sources Discussed

Current contents: Social & behavioral sciences. (1969–present). Philadelphia: Institute for Scientific Information. Weekly.

American Psychological Association. (1987–present. *PsycSCAN: Applied experimental & engineering psychology.* Washington, DC: Author. Quarterly.

American Psychological Association. (1981–present). *PsycSCAN: Applied psychology.* Washington, DC: Author. Quarterly.

American Psychological Association. (1980–present). *PsycSCAN: Clinical psychology.* Washington, DC: Author. Quarterly.

American Psychological Association. (1980–present). *PsycSCAN: Developmental psychology.* Washington, DC: Author. Quarterly.

American Psychological Association. (1982–present). *PsycSCAN: LD/MR.* Washington, DC: Author. Quarterly.

American Psychological Association. (1986–present). *PsycSCAN: Psychoanalysis.* Washington, DC: Author. Quarterly.

The well-read psychologist may identify many journals in which major, interesting studies are routinely published. Unfortunately, he or she often cannot afford a subscription to each journal of interest. Current-awareness tools help the researcher keep abreast of recently published research. The previously mentioned indexing tools, such as *Psychological Abstracts,* are preferred for retrospective literature searching because they provide a comprehensive list of sources relevant to a topic and include extensive indexes. In contrast, current-awareness services usually do not provide detailed indexing. But they supplement a retrospective literature review by offering two important conveniences. First, they provide timely access to journal literature because, in some cases, they can be produced more quickly than indexing tools can. Second, the researcher can quickly scan the contents of those journals that he or she has identified as regularly containing articles of interest or on topics under investigation.

One such tool, *Current Contents: Social & Behavioral Sciences (CC),* reproduces the tables of contents from about 1,300 journals in the social and behavioral sciences around the world. Each journal issue's table of contents provides article titles, authors' names, and the page number on which each article begins. Because of the production process employed, *CC* is extremely timely: Issues of *CC* are compiled and sent to subscribers weekly. Thus, within a few weeks of the publication of a journal article, the *CC* reader is made aware of the article's availability. In addition to providing timely access to journal contents, *CC* allows the researcher to browse the contents of many journal issues of possible interest. The Institute for Scientific Information publishes several *CC* series covering other groups of disciplines: for example, Life Sciences, Clinical Medicine, Arts & Humanities. In addition to paper issues, some subject-specific editions of CC may be received on diskette to be used with the researcher's personal computer.

Figure 10–A illustrates the organization of a *Current Contents: Social & Behavioral Sciences* issue. Journals are grouped under

FIGURE 10-A

Selected sections from the table of contents of *Current Contents: Social & Behavioral Sciences* (Vol. 22, issue 28, July 9, 1990) and the table of contents of *International Journal of Man–Machine Studies* (p. 47).

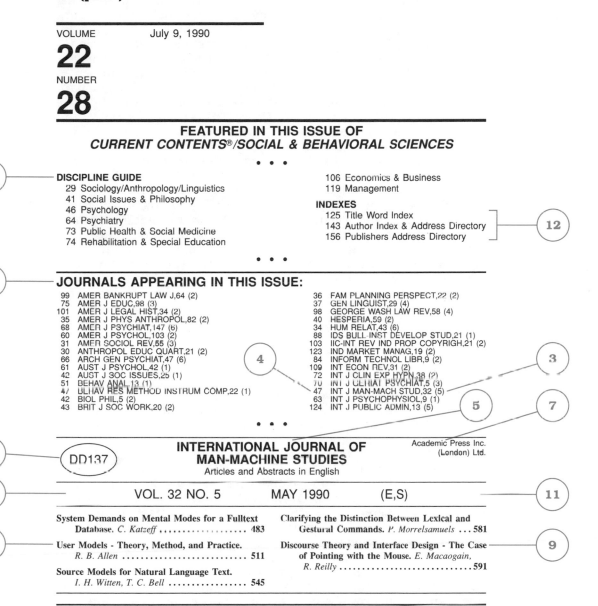

VOLUME July 9, 1990

22

NUMBER

28

FEATURED IN THIS ISSUE OF
CURRENT CONTENTS®/SOCIAL & BEHAVIORAL SCIENCES

• • •

DISCIPLINE GUIDE
29 Sociology/Anthropology/Linguistics
41 Social Issues & Philosophy
46 Psychology
64 Psychiatry
73 Public Health & Social Medicine
74 Rehabilitation & Special Education

106 Economics & Business
119 Management

INDEXES
125 Title Word Index
143 Author Index & Address Directory
156 Publishers Address Directory

• • •

JOURNALS APPEARING IN THIS ISSUE:

99   AMER BANKRUPT LAW J,64 (2)
75   AMER J EDUC,98 (3)
101 AMER J LEGAL HIST,34 (2)
35   AMER J PHYS ANTHROPOL,82 (2)
68   AMER J PSYCHIAT,147 (6)
60   AMER J PSYCHOL,103 (2)
31   AMER SOCIOL REV,55 (3)
30   ANTHROPOL EDUC QUART,21 (2)
66   ARCH GEN PSYCHIAT,47 (6)
61   AUST J PSYCHOL,42 (1)
42   AUST J SOC ISSUES,25 (1)
51   BEHAV ANAL,13 (1)
47   BEHAV RES METHOD INSTRUM COMP,22 (1)
42   BIOL PHIL,5 (2)
43   BRIT J SOC WORK,20 (2)

36   FAM PLANNING PERSPECT,22 (2)
37   GEN LINGUIST,29 (4)
98   GEORGE WASH LAW REV,58 (4)
40   HESPERIA,59 (2)
34   HUM RELAT,43 (4)
88   IDS BULL-INST DEVELOP STUD,21 (1)
103 IIC-INT REV IND PROP COPYRIGH,21 (2)
123 IND MARKET MANAG,19 (2)
84   INFORM TECHNOL LIBR,9 (2)
109 INT ECON REV,31 (2)
72   INT J CLIN EXP HYPN,38 (2)
70   INT J CLINAT PSYCHIAT,5 (3)
47   INT J MAN-MACH STUD,32 (5)
63   INT J PSYCHOPHYSIOL,9 (1)
124 INT J PUBLIC ADMIN,13 (5)

• • •

INTERNATIONAL JOURNAL OF
MAN-MACHINE STUDIES
Articles and Abstracts in English

Academic Press Inc.
(London) Ltd.

DD137

| VOL. 32 NO. 5 | MAY 1990 | (E,S) |

System Demands on Mental Modes for a Fulltext Database. *C. Katzeff* 483

User Models - Theory, Method, and Practice. *R. B. Allen* 511

Source Models for Natural Language Text. *I. H. Witten, T. C. Bell* 545

Clarifying the Distinction Between Lexical and Gestural Commands. *P. Morrelsamuels* ... 581

Discourse Theory and Interface Design - The Case of Pointing with the Mouse. *E. Macaogain, R. Reilly* 581

broad subject areas (**1**), such as psychology, psychiatry, education (not shown), and management, allowing the user to browse by subject areas. In the process of our literature review on human-computer interaction, we discovered that *International Journal of Man-Machine Studies* publishes a considerable amount in this area. However, we need to find studies that are more recent than those that have appeared in *Psychological Abstracts.* Therefore, we consult each *CC* issue, beginning with the most current and working back in time. (Because most journals are not published as frequently as *CC*, not all journal titles will be included in each issue.) An index in the front of each *CC* issue lists the names of the journals included that week and the page on which their tables of contents are reproduced (**2**). In Figure 10–A, we find that Volume 32, issue 5 of *International Journal of Man–Machine Studies* (**3**) is included in this issue of *CC* on page 47 (**4**). Turning to this page, we find the table of contents for this journal (**5**) and issue number (**6**) reproduced. Also included in this entry is the name of the journal's publisher, Academic Press (**7**). This issue contains two articles of potential interest to our topic: "User Models—Theory, Method, and Practice" by R. B. Allen (**8**), and "Discourse Theory and Interface Design" by E. Macaogain and R. Reilly (**9**).

CC provides two pieces of additional information. In conjunction with all the *CC* publications, the Institute for Scientific Information provides a document delivery service called the Genuine Article. For a fee, this service will provide copies of articles covered in any of the *Current Contents* publications. This might be useful if a journal is not owned by a local library and you cannot wait for interlibrary loan services (see chapter 11). A unique number representing this journal title and issue is provided (**10**) should you wish to use this service. As indicated above, there are several *CC* publications, each covering particular subject areas. Each table of contents contains codes indicating other *CC* publications in which a journal title is included (**11**). In this case, *International Journal of Man–Machine Studies* is included in the weekly *Current Contents: Engineering* (E) and, as we already know, the *Social & Behavioral Sciences* (S).

It is important to emphasize that if you want to use *CC* effectively, you must be familiar with journal titles that routinely publish articles on your topic and you must be willing to scan *CC* regularly. Each weekly issue of *CC* contains an Author Index, a Publishers Address Directory, and a Title Word Index (**12**). The last is a subject index composed of significant words appearing in article titles.

A similar series is *PsycSCAN*, published quarterly by the American Psychological Association. Whereas *CC* provides access to journals representing a wide range of disciplines, *PsycSCAN* limits coverage to journals of potential interest to psychologists. Presently there are six separate *PsycSCAN* publications, each covering a select set of journals in a particular subject area: *Applied Experimental & Engineering Psychology, Applied Psychology, Clinical Psychology, Developmental Psychology, Learning Disabilities/Mental Retardation,* and *Psychoanalysis.* Although not as timely as *CC*, this series has several advantages. A researcher can subscribe to one source that provides coverage in a particular area of interest. Each journal-article entry in *PsycSCAN* contains the bibliographic information and article abstract exactly as they appear in *Psychological Abstracts.* Although the completeness of each entry reduces *PsycSCAN*'s effectiveness as a timely current-awareness tool, the nonevaluative summaries can help you separate the truly relevant current journal literature from those with enticing, but occasionally misleading, titles.

The publication covering the general area of human-computer interaction is *PsycSCAN: Applied Experimental & Engineering Psychology.* This *PsycSCAN* organizes citations and abstracts under broad subject areas. The two most appropriate to our topic are *Man–Machine Systems* and *Man–Machine Systems Design.*

Dissertations

Sources Discussed

Dissertation abstracts international. Part A: Humanities and social sciences. Part B: Sciences and engineering. (1938–present). Ann Arbor, MI: University Microfilms International (UMI). Monthly. *Part C: Worldwide.* (1976–present). Ann Arbor, MI: UMI. Quarterly.

Comprehensive dissertation index. (1973–present). Ann Arbor, MI: UMI. Annual. Retrospective set covers 1861–1972.

As we discussed in chapter 4, doctoral dissertations are the result of original research and as such constitute an important body of literature in psychology. In the past, you could use *Psychological Abstracts* to identify doctoral dissertations in psychology. However, since 1980, dissertations have been included only in the machine-readable version of *Psychological Abstracts* (that is, *PsycINFO*), not in the print *PA*. In addition, neither the database nor the print sources provide abstracts for dissertations. Dissertation citations also appear in other indexing sources, both print and machine readable. Therefore, uncovering citations to several dissertations in a search is not unusual. Most doctoral dissertations are unpublished and therefore difficult to obtain, and many libraries do not purchase dissertations as a matter of policy. Because you can spend $30 or more to purchase a single dissertation, you should, for the sake of economy, determine as much about the scope and content of the dissertation as possible.

Universities granting doctoral degrees retain only a few copies of a dissertation, and these must be used in the library or in another archive. Therefore, they are difficult to borrow or obtain on interlibrary loan. In order to announce their availability to researchers, copies of most doctoral dissertations written in the United States are sent to University Microfilms International (UMI). Upon receipt of a dissertation, UMI microfilms it and announces its availability in *Dissertation Abstracts International (DAI)*. UMI also sells copies of dissertations in microfilm and paper formats.

DAI is published in three parts: Part A, *The Humanities and Social Sciences;* Part B, *The Sciences and Engineering;* and Part C, *Worldwide.* Parts A and B include references to approximately 35,000 dissertations each year produced at American, Canadian, and British institutions of higher education. Part C includes dissertations from other countries.

Although the broad area of psychology is covered in Part B, as a science, other research of interest to psychologists may be covered in Part A. Some of these areas are educational psychology, testing and measurement, gerontology, and so forth. Each monthly issue of Parts A and B contains a *keyword subject index,* which indexes dissertations by significant words in the title, and an author index.

Within each monthly issue, dissertations are listed under broad discipline areas and thereunder by subtopic; for example, psychology is listed along with several subtopics such as general, developmental, industrial, and psychometrics. However, dissertations in interdisciplinary areas could appear in more than one category. For

FIGURE 10-B

Portions of the Keyword Subject Index (p. 74) and Author Index (p. 4), and a citation and abstract by Bonnie Elizabeth John (p. 5551-B), from *Dissertation Abstracts International. Part B: The Sciences and Engineering* (Vol. 49 issue 12, June 1989).

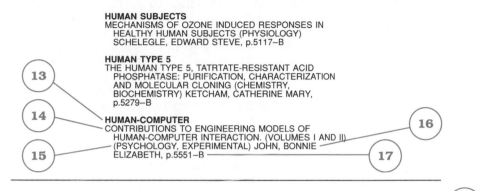

HUMAN SUBJECTS
MECHANISMS OF OZONE INDUCED RESPONSES IN HEALTHY HUMAN SUBJECTS (PHYSIOLOGY) SCHELEGLE, EDWARD STEVE, p.5117–B

HUMAN TYPE 5
THE HUMAN TYPE 5, TATRTATE-RESISTANT ACID PHOSPHATASE: PURIFICATION, CHARACTERIZATION AND MOLECULAR CLONING (CHEMISTRY, BIOCHEMISTRY) KETCHAM, CATHERINE MARY, p.5279–B

HUMAN-COMPUTER
CONTRIBUTIONS TO ENGINEERING MODELS OF HUMAN-COMPUTER INTERACTION. (VOLUMES I AND II) (PSYCHOLOGY, EXPERIMENTAL) JOHN, BONNIE ELIZABETH, p.5551–B

PSYCHOLOGY, EXPERIMENTAL

Contributions to engineering models of human-computer interaction. (Volumes I and II). John, Bonnie Elizabeth, Ph.D. *Carnegie-Mellon University,* 1988. 301pp.

Order Number DA8904838

This dissertation presents two engineering models of behavior at the human-computer interface; a model of immediate behavior and stimulus-response compatibility and a model of transcription typing. Formulated within the architecture of the Model Human Processor of Card, Moran and Newell, these models are able to make zero-parameter, quantitative predictions of human response time in their respective domains. They are also completely integrated, making good predictions about performance on a dual reaction-time/typing task. Parameters of the models are set using response time data from an abbreviation recall experiment. These parameters are then used to make predictions about response time in another abbreviation recall experiment, three classic stimulus-response experiments, and over 29 experiments that reflect robust phenomena associated with transcription typing. These models are the first to make successful predictions across domain boundaries, both within tasks exhibiting stimulus-response compatibility and outside that paradigm to transcription typing.

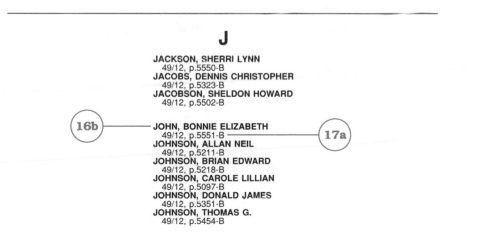

J

JACKSON, SHERRI LYNN
    49/12, p.5550-B
JACOBS, DENNIS CHRISTOPHER
    49/12, p.5323-B
JACOBSON, SHELDON HOWARD
    49/12, p.5502-B

JOHN, BONNIE ELIZABETH
    49/12, p.5551-B
JOHNSON, ALLAN NEIL
    49/12, p.5211-B
JOHNSON, BRIAN EDWARD
    49/12, p.5218-B
JOHNSON, CAROLE LILLIAN
    49/12, p.5097-B
JOHNSON, DONALD JAMES
    49/12, p.5351-B
JOHNSON, THOMAS G.
    49/12, p.5454-B

example, some aspects of human–computer interaction could be included in the section covering engineering. The broad categories also make browsing for titles inconvenient. Therefore, we start by using the key word index in the current monthly issues of *DAI*, Part B.

Figure 10–B illustrates two approaches to *DAI*. Using the key-word subject approach, we find one entry under the phrase *human–computer* (**13**). (As with any keyword index, it is advisable to check under several synonyms to avoid missing relevant material.) The entry under this subject consists of the title of the dissertation (**14**), the subject area (**15**), and the name of the author (**16**). The abstract appears on page 5551-B (**17**). Turning to this page, the dissertation title (**14a**), author (**16a**), institution granting the degree (**18**), and year in which the degree was awarded (**19**) appear at the beginning of the entry. Following this information is a lengthy abstract (**20**) composed by the author that describes the dissertation.

As discussed earlier in this section, copies of dissertations are sold by UMI; in many cases, this is the only way that a copy may be obtained. Should you wish to purchase this title, an order number (**21**) is provided. You may photocopy order forms from recent monthly issues of *DAI*.

Monthly issues of *DAI* also contain an author index. Had we known that Bonnie Elizabeth John had written this dissertation, we could have used this index to find this same dissertation. Under the author entry (**16b**), we find that the full entry with abstract appears in Volume 49, issue 12, page 5551-B of *DAI* (**17a**). The author indexes for all 12 issues of *DAI* cumulate in the last issue of the volume.

When searching for dissertations by subject, combing the monthly indexes for both parts of *DAI* can be time-consuming. The annual *Comprehensive Dissertation Index,* which is published as a five-volume companion to *DAI* Parts A and B, provides a partial solution. Volumes 1 and 2 have indexes for subjects in the sciences: agriculture, chemistry, health sciences, engineering, and so forth. Volumes 3 and 4 include indexes for the humanities and social sciences; in this case, psychology. There is a combined author index in Volume 5.

In addition, like many other sources discussed elsewhere in this book, *DAI* is available in machine-readable, CD-ROM format.

Biographical Information

Sources Discussed

American Psychological Association. (1948–present). *Directory of the American Psychological Association.* Washington, DC: Author. Quadrennial.

American Psychological Association. (1967–present). *APA Membership Register.* Washington, DC: Author. Annual (in years the *Directory* is not published).

Who's who in America. (2 vols.). (1899/1900–present). Chicago: Marquis Who's Who. Biennial.

Who was who in America. (1943–present). Chicago: Marquis Who's Who. Irregular. Historical volume covering 1607 to 1896, plus volumes bringing coverage up to 1985.

History of psychology in autobiography (Vols. 1–4). (1930–1952). New York: Russell & Russell.

(Vol. 5). (1967). New York: Appleton-Century-Crofts.

(Vol. 6). (1974). Englewood Cliffs, NJ: Prentice-Hall

(Vol. 7). (1980). San Francisco: W. H. Freeman.

(Vol. 8). (1989). Stanford, CA: Stanford University Press.

Directories

Biographical directories can serve many purposes. They may provide current mailing addresses, lists of academic credentials, recent publications, and personal information. This may ease professional correspondence or be useful for evaluating research by a particular author. Information on a psychologist's current research activities, credentials, and previous publications can be used to determine if an author has the background appropriate to the topic discussed in a journal article or book.

There are hundreds of biographical directories, each providing a different type of information and scope of coverage. Consequently, in this section we discuss a highly selective list of sources and focus on one that illustrates the type of information represented in many biographical directories.

The primary purpose of the *Directory of the American Psychological Association (Directory)* is to provide brief biographical data on APA members. Data are solicited by questionnaires sent to the membership.

As mentioned earlier in this chapter, Donald A. Norman, a cognitive psychologist, has written a great deal in the area of human–computer interaction. We might want to know more about his educational background and credentials. He may be an APA member, so we turn first to the *Directory* for some brief biographical information. We find an entry from the 1989 *Directory*, as illustrated in Figure 10–C. Individuals are listed by surname in the Roster section (**22**). Included in each entry are an institutional or business mailing address (**23**) and telephone number (**24**). The amount of additional information varies and can include date of birth (**25**), highest educational degree earned (**26**), major field of current research interest (**27**), and specialty areas within this field (**28**). His position, current at the time that this information was provided,

FIGURE 10-C

Entry for Donald A. Norman from the *Directory of the American Psychological Association* (1989 Edition, Vol. II, p. 863).

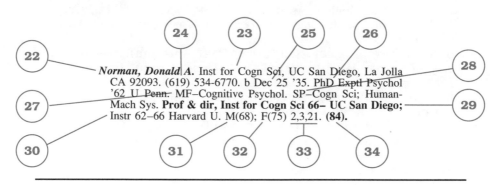

was professor and director at the Institute for Cognitive Science at University of California at San Diego; this is noted in boldface type (**29**), as well a previous institutional affiliation with Harvard University (**30**). He has been a member of APA since 1968 (**31**) and a Fellow of the Association since 1975 (**32**). The numbers that follow (**33**) indicate the APA divisions to which Donald Norman belongs: Teaching of Psychology (Division 2), Experimental Psychology (Division 3), and Applied Experimental and Engineering Psychologists (Division 21). The date in parentheses indicates the year that this information was last updated (**34**). For some individuals, more information is provided. A guide to additional information is provided in the front of each edition of the *Directory*.

This entry also illustrates a limitation of biographical directories. It appeared in the 1989 *Directory*, based on information supplied by the biographee in 1984. By 1991, Donald Norman's position was chair of the Department of Cognitive Science at University of California at San Diego. Although biographical information of a historical nature remains the same, the more current information in such directories is subject to change.

The *Directory* also contains a Geographical Index and an index by divisional membership. In addition to providing information on individuals, the *Directory* contains a number of documents of interest to psychologists. Among these are statistics on APA membership, statements of principles and standards of professional practice, a synopsis of laws related to practice of psychology in the United States and Canada, and the Association's bylaws. Published in years when the *Directory* is not published, the *APA Membership Register (Register)* provides updated mailing addresses.

The *Directory* and *Register* are two of the most important information sources on psychologists working in the United States. The *International Directory of Psychologists* (Pawlik, 1985) provides similar information for psychologists working abroad. Although individuals from 51 countries are listed, some countries received better coverage than others.

Almost every country is represented by a national biographical publication containing data on the country's more accomplished citizens, although the comprehensiveness and frequency of these publications vary. One example is *Who's Who in America*, which contains vital statistics on prominent living Americans. *Who Was Who in America* offers similar brief biographical information on deceased Americans.

Other Sources

The *History of Psychology in Autobiography* presents a series of lengthy autobiographical essays by some of the most influential American psychologists. Each essay includes the life history of the person profiled as well as discussions of the person's important research and selected bibliographies of his or her publications. Because the essays reflect the psychologist's view of his or her research and of the discipline as a whole, they provide unique insights into each psychologist both as an individual and as a professional. Eminent psychologists included are, for example, S. S. Stevens, B. F. Skinner, G. W. Allport, R. S. Woodworth, R. M. Yerkes, L. J. Cronbach, and E. E. Maccoby. If you are a student of the history of psychology, this source may be of special interest to you.

T. S. Krawiec (1972, 1974, 1978) provides a similar set of autobiographical essays on 35 psychologists. Each person included is distinguished by his or her contributions through teaching, research, or writing. People included are, for example, A. Anastasi, R. B. Cattell, H. Helson, W. J. McKeachie, C. E. Osgood, P. Suppes, and R. I. Watson.

The Women of Psychology (Stevens & Gardner, 1982) contains biographies of 137 individuals. Although not all biographees are psychologists by training, all made significant contributions to the development of psychological theory and research. Among those included are F. L. Goodenough, L. S. Hollingworth, and L. Bender.

D. L. Sills (1979) includes biographies of 215 persons from the social sciences. Those selected for inclusion were major and influential forces in their respective fields. Essays were written by prominent academics in each field. Extensive bibliographies accompany each article.

Book Reviews

Sources Discussed

Contemporary psychology. (1956–present). Washington, DC: American Psychological Association. Monthly.

Book review index. (1965–present). Detroit: Gale Research. Bimonthly.

Book reviews appearing in professional journals serve many purposes. Some faculty use reviews for selecting textbooks for college courses. Researchers regularly scan reviews for important new books in their fields of interest and to keep abreast of revised and updated editions of older publications. You may find reviews useful for evaluating a book's content and for placing it in the context of other available literature. Ideally, reviews are not limited to a description of a book's contents and a statement of recommendation or censure. Reviewers for scholarly journals are usually academics who are well acquainted with the literature in their respective fields. Therefore, they are able to evaluate a particular book in relation to other available literature.

The purpose of *Contemporary Psychology* is to provide evaluative reviews of current psychology materials. Although emphasis is on books of interest to psychologists and their students, films, tapes, and other media are also included. Each issue contains lengthy reviews (between one and two pages) of approximately 55 titles and brief reviews of between 10 and 20 additional titles. Books are critiqued on their own merits and evaluated in relation to existing psychological literature and thought. Each December issue contains an index, arranged by authors' and reviewers' names, to all reviews published during the year.

Having read Donald Norman's *The Psychology of Everyday Things* and found some information about the author, the next step might be to determine how someone else in the field of human–computer interaction views the book and its contribution to the literature. By searching the annual *Contemporary Psychology* indexes, we find a review in the October 1989 issue. Part of the review, under the title "The Cognitive Psychology of Usable Artifacts" (**35**) is reproduced in Figure 10–D. Basic bibliographic information about the book is provided (**36**), as well as the name of the reviewer (**37**). The review begins with some brief biographical information about Donald Norman (**38**) and the credentials of the reviewer, David E. Kieras (**39**).

Reviews appearing in *Contemporary Psychology* and in more than 400 other scholarly journals and general-interest magazines are indexed in *Book Review Index.* Citations are arranged by book author or editor and by title. The number of journals and popular magazines indexed and the range of disciplines covered provide an excellent starting point for accessing book-review citations.

Two of the indexing sources described in chapter 5 include separate sections for citations to book reviews. In the back of each monthly issue and annual cumulation of *Education Index* and *Business Periodicals Index,* reviews are listed by book author.

FIGURE 10–D
Portions of a review of *The Psychology of Everyday Things* from *Contemporary Psychology* (Vol. 34, issue 10, October 1989, p. 914).

(35)

The Cognitive Psychology of Usable Artifacts

(36)

Donald A. Norman
The Psychology of Everyday Things
New York: Basic Books, 1988. 257 pp.
ISBN 0-465-06709-3. $19.95

Review by
David E. Kieras

(37)

(38)

Donald A. Norman, professor of psychology and cognitive science and chair of the Department for Cognitive Science at the University of California (San Diego), is author of Learning and Memory. ■ *David E. Kieras, associate professor of electrical engineering and computer science at the University of Michigan (Ann Arbor), is author of the chapter "What Mental Model Should Be Taught: Choosing Instructional Content for Complex Engineered Systems" in J. Psotka, L. D. Massey, and S. Mutter (Eds.)* Intelligent Tutoring Systems: Lessons Learned.

(39)

We humans live in a world that is occupied by many thousands of artifacts that we use in our everyday lives to get along in our world and all of which have been designed by fellow humans. Norman's thesis is that many of these everyday devices are poorly designed and could be improved. This book is a polemic on the design failures of everyday artifacts, along with some recommendations for how they could be designed better. The most fascinating content is the many examples of poor design of everyday objects, such as door handles and faucets.

This book is basically a popularization of some of the practical implications of cognitive psychology. As a popularization, the book should be judged by how the general public accepts and responds

concerns of making our world an easier place in which to live and for scientific investigations of how people construct and get along in environments. The intense interest in human–computer interaction shared by many cognitive psychologists is an example of such concerns. However, what is especially interesting and inspiring about this book is that it shows how such issues arise not just with high-technology equipment such as computers, but also with telephones and light switches. Norman's book thus provides the important service of pointing out where psychology, in the form of applied cognitive psychology or "cognitive engineering," can make some real contributions to the everyday practical world. It also opens a new and fascinating area of research.

• • •   • • •

References

Booth, P. (1989). *An introduction to human-computer interaction.* Hillsdale, NJ: Lawrence Erlbaum.

Card, S. K., Moran, T. P., & Newell, A. (1983). *The psychology of human-computer interaction.* Hillsdale, NJ: Lawrence Erlbaum.

Kantowitz, B. H., & Sorkin, R. D. (1983). *Human factors: Understanding people–system relationships.* New York: Wiley.

Krawiec, T. S. (1972,1974,1978). *The psychologists* (Vols. 1–3). New York: Oxford University Press.

Newell, A., & Card, S. (1986). Straightening out softening up: Response to Carroll and Campbell. *Human-Computer Interaction, 2,* 227–249.

Norman, D. A. (1983). Design rules based on analyses of human error. *Communications of the ACM, 26,* 254–258.

Norman, D. A. (1988). *The psychology of everyday things.* New York: Basic Books.

Norman, D. A., & Draper, S. W. (1986). *User centered system design.* Hillsdale, NJ: Lawrence Erlbaum.

Pawlik, K. (Ed.). (1985). *International directory of psychologists, exclusive of the U.S.A..* Amsterdam, Netherlands: Elsevier Science.

Sanders, M. S., & McCormick, E. J. (1987). *Human factors in engineering and design* (5th ed.). New York: McGraw-Hill.

Shneiderman, B. (1987). *Designing the user interface: Strategies for effective human-computer interaction.* Reading, MA: Addison-Wesley.

Sills, D. L. (Ed.). (1979). *International encyclopedia of the social sciences: Biographical supplement.* New York: Free Press.

Smith, D. C., Irby, C., Kimball, R., Verplank, B., & Harslem, E. (1982, April). Designing the Star user inferface. *BYTE,* 242–282.

Stevens, G, and Gardner, S. (1982). *The women of psychology* (Vols. 1–2). Cambridge, MA: Schenkman.

Van Cott, H. P., & Kinkade, R. G. (1972). *Human engineering guide to equipment design.* Washington, DC: U.S. Goverment Printing Office.

11 It's Not in the Library

You have used indexes, abstracts, and other sources to compile a list of citations to relevant journal articles, books, and other materials. You have found some of these by checking the card or online catalog, the journal collection, government documents, and other resources. But your library may not own all of the research materials you need. This situation is not unusual. Because of the space needed for book, journal, and document storage and the high costs associated with purchase of books and subscriptions to journals, no library is able to own all of the materials needed for research by its community of faculty, students, and staff. This situation is true for small college libraries as well as large, research-oriented university libraries.

After exhausting the resources of your library, then, where can you obtain additional materials? There are several options. Among these are interlibrary loan, travel to other libraries, and document purchase.

Chapter Example: Selective Attention

Attention is the focusing of cognitive or mental activity. Selective attention is a process in which we focus on one or a few stimuli, on some aspects of those stimuli, or on a particular task, while ignoring other stimuli or tasks (Broadbent, 1958; Crooks & Stein, 1988; Matlin, 1983). In other words, we do not attend equally to all stimulus inputs which the brain receives.

Why is this important? We are continually presented with numerous stimuli of many different types (both external and internal) to which we could attend. External stimuli include those generated by the environment itself (e.g., noises or foul odors), messages in the environment generated by humans to which we are exposed (e.g., signs), and stimuli to which we choose to expose ourselves (e.g., conversations or music). Internal stimuli include those generated by our bodies (e.g., headache, tight shoes, or breathing). Shiffrin (1986) notes that there are limits upon our attentional resources. Our brains could not possibly attend meaningfully to all of the many stimuli available at any point in time. Some tasks may be so complex that they require a significant degree of concentration for comprehension; for example, reading and understanding this book. The process of selective attention allows us to focus on particular sources of information.

Numerous questions have been asked about selective attention, including the following: What are the limits of attention? To what extent is it possible to divide one's attention among several things simultaneously? What causes attention to shift? How quickly can we change our focus of attention? (Johnston & Dark, 1986; Shiffrin, 1986) Much research has been conducted on selective attention over the past few decades. Students are frequently introduced to some of the more interesting research; for example, the cocktail party effect and the Stroop effect.

The cocktail party effect, described by Cherry (1953) and demonstrated in the film *Information Processing* (CRM, 1971) is concerned with the conflict between focused and divided attention. One can focus on a particular set of stimuli, such as a conversation at a cocktail party, yet become aware of and process important information contained in other stimuli, such as one's name, which may cause a change in the focus of attention. But how can our attention be focused and divided simultaneously? What are the limits on selective attention? These questions have been pursued by researchers for many years.

A classic example of the failure of attention through interference, the Stroop effect (MacLeod, 1991; Stroop, 1935), is typically demonstrated using the Stroop Color Word task. In a typical stimulus configuration, selected words for colors are presented in randomly colored inks or randomly colored backgrounds; for example, "red" may be presented in blue or red ink on a blue or red background. A subject's task may be to read the word or to say the color of the word. Competition between the relevant and irrelevant stimuli (the word and its color) within the focus of attention causes errors. Presentation of information has been manipulated in numerous experiments separating relevant from irrelevant information.

The questions and research noted above focus on normal human behavior. However, consider what happens when there is a failure of attention processes. Attention deficit disorder (ADD, also known as attention deficit hyperactivity disorder) in children is an example. ADD is characterized by behavioral factors such as easy distractability, difficulty playing quietly, difficulty sustaining attention, and frequent shifting of attention from one uncompleted task to another (American Psychiatric Association, 1987). Although they may be normal in other respects, children with ADD have difficulty getting things done and difficulty getting along with others. Such children often have problems in school and at home. The cause of ADD is not known, yet partial potential explanations have included genetic factors (Biederman et al., 1986) and abnormal glucose metabolism (Zametkin et al., 1990). Effective treatment strategies have included both pharmacological and behavioral therapies (Henker & Whalen, 1989).

In this chapter, we will use selective attention as our sample topic to demonstrate retrieving information not available in your local library.

Interlibrary Loan

Libraries willing to assist one another in meeting the information needs of their users belong to one or more library networks that involve reciprocal agreements between libraries. Through these networks, a library may be able to obtain for one of its users a journal article, a book, or another publication that it does not own. Because of these networks, you may have access to a library located in another city or another state through a service known as *interlibrary loan* (ILL).

ILL policies vary among libraries. Each library establishes its own guidelines based upon local funding, staffing, and other priorities. An ILL librarian or a reference librarian will be able to inform you about local library policies. If you decide to use this service, you must keep in mind several things.

First, ILL takes time. Seldom can you obtain materials in less than two weeks. A rare journal or a book owned by only a few libraries (as may be the case for materials published in other countries or by small publishing houses) may involve a wait of a month or more. Thus you must begin your search early. Allow time to compile a list of references, to check your library's holdings, and to request materials through ILL. Once you receive these materials, you will need time to read and analyze them and to write your report.

Second, ILL procedures differ from library to library. Some libraries provide this service only to faculty members or to faculty and graduate students. Some networks do not provide services for student users. Therefore you must inquire about whether ILL is available to you.

Third, you must provide complete bibliographic information for the materials you wish to request. Such provision will not be a problem if you have consistently and accurately noted all the information you have found in an index or abstract entry. If you have not, you will need to retrace literature search steps to fill in the gaps in bibliographic information for each item requested.

Finally, some libraries charge for ILL service, especially for journal article requests. Libraries seldom lend an entire issue or a volume of a journal. Instead the article you need will be photocopied and mailed to your library. The cost of photocopying the article, any service charge for locating the material, postage, and so forth may be passed on to you.

Typical ILL Procedures

After checking library policies, your next step is to decide what materials you really need to request. Given the time involved and possible monetary charges, you must identify essential sources and separate them from the nonessential (tangential, trivial, or redundant). Information contained in the abstracting and reviewing sources discussed in earlier chapters will help you evaluate the potential relevance of materials.

Once you have determined what materials you need, you must complete an ILL request form for each article, book, or other document. You can obtain this form from a reference or interlibrary-loan librarian. Your completed form will be the library's record of your request. Keep a record of materials that you have requested. Such a record will prevent duplicate requests, save you time and money, and let you know what material to expect.

To illustrate a book request, we use one of the references identified in the *Annual Review of Psychology* chapter on selective attention (Johnston & Dark, 1986). Figure 11–A illustrates the ILL request for this book, *Perceptual Organization*. You must provide complete bibliographic information, including the names of the authors or editors (**1**), the book title and subtitle if there is one (**2**), the place of publication (**3**), the name of the publisher (**4**), and the date of publication (**5**). In addition, the source in which the bibliographic information was located is requested (**6**). Some libraries will not process a request if information on the source is incomplete or omitted. Other information includes the date on which the request was placed (**7**) and the date after which the book will no longer be useful for your research (**8**). Additionally, there is space on the form for information identifying the person making the request (**9**). The form your library uses may be slightly different, but it will probably require the same kind of information.

One of the sources that we used to update the journal references in the *Annual Review of Psychology* article was *PsycLIT*, a machine-readable version of *Psychological Abstracts*. Among the references we found was an article by A. H. Van der Heijden in the *Canadian Journal of Psychology*. Figure 11–B presents a sample ILL request card completed for this article. As with the book request, you must provide complete bibliographic information: the name(s) of the author(s) (**10**), the article title (**11**), the journal title (**12**), the year of publication (**13**), the volume number (**14**), the issue and month (**15**), and the pages on which the article appears (**16**). The source of the bibliographic information is again requested (**17**), along with the date after which you no longer need the article (**18**). You may also be asked to provide the amount you are willing to pay for the duplication of the article (**19**). Note that in many respects the forms for book and journal requests are similar.

After submitting your request(s), inquire about notification procedures. Will the library telephone or write to you? Must you contact the library after a reasonable period of time to see if the materials

FIGURE 11-A

An interlibrary-loan book request form.

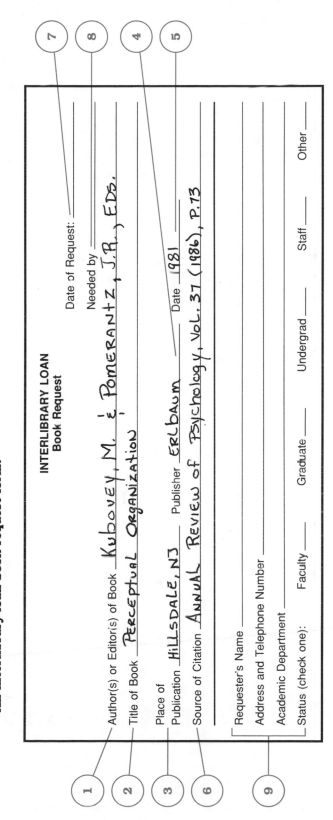

INTERLIBRARY LOAN
Book Request

Date of Request: _____

Needed by _____

Author(s) or Editor(s) of Book _Kubovey, M. & Pomerantz, J.R., Eds._

Title of Book _Perceptual Organization_

Place of
Publication _Hillsdale, NJ_   Publisher _Erlbaum_   Date _1981_

Source of Citation _Annual Review of Psychology, Vol. 37 (1986), p.73_

Requester's Name _____

Address and Telephone Number _____

Academic Department _____

Status (check one):   Faculty _____   Graduate _____   Undergrad _____   Staff _____   Other _____

FIGURE 11-B
An interlibrary-loan journal article request form.

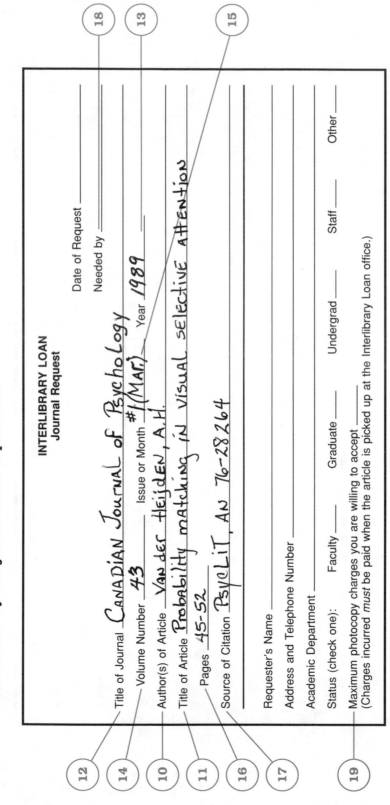

have been received? Also inquire about billing procedures and an estimated date of receipt of materials.

Why does the ILL procedure consume so much time? Your request takes a tortuous journey involving many steps. Take the example of a journal-article request. A staff member will first locate information about the requested journal through a standard bibliographic source and identify a library that reports owning the journal. A request form will then be prepared and sent electronically or by mail to the lending library. Staff in the lending library will locate the material, make a copy of the article, prepare the bill, and mail the photocopy to your requesting library. The requesting library may then contact you. In this procedure, delays and problems may occur. If you have provided incomplete or inaccurate information, your request will probably wait while other requests with complete information are processed. A rare or obscure source may be hard to locate. The needed article may be missing from the library that is contacted. Any number of people involved in the process may make a mistake, or the source that indicated that a particular library has your journal may be wrong. A holiday, an ill staff member, or a malfunctioning photocopier can also delay the process. Even without delays and problems, any procedure involving the mail requires time. The bottom line is—allow plenty of time! With adequate planning, the ILL services available to you will meet almost all of your information needs not met by the local library.

Travel to Other Libraries

In some circumstances, you may want to travel to another library to use materials. For example, you may be unable to wait for interlibrary loan. In most cases, libraries will not loan reference books, entire journal issues or volumes, or dissertations. Therefore, you may have to use a library that owns the material you need. Fortunately, computerized cataloging networks let librarians locate books and journal titles for you, whether they are in the same city or state, or across the country.

The most extensive network is the Online Computer Library Center (OCLC). This database represents many holdings for books and journals of over 4,000 libraries. A smaller, more specialized network is the Research Libraries Information Network (RLIN), which comprises large research libraries. Libraries use such networks and their computerized records to share cataloging information and obtain records for their own card or online catalogs. Librarians also use the network to locate books and journals for interlibrary loan. On request, they may provide you with a list of locations holding a book or journal title you need. In most cases, you may be able to use materials you need at the library owning them, although you will not be able to borrow them.

This alternative must be used with caution, however. You will not be able to write or call other libraries and request that the materials be sent to you. Libraries provide photocopy and loan services only to other libraries, not to individuals. In addition, these networks do not provide circulation information for books and journals. Therefore, you may find that the volume you need is signed out, missing, or not on the shelf for a variety of reasons. Some institutions restrict the use of their facilities: You may have to produce an identification card to gain access to the library.

The options at your disposal will continue to increase as more library functions become computerized. For example, some libraries are able to access the computerized catalogs of other libraries in addition to their own, in much the same way that they search the bibliographic databases described in chapter 8. For accurate and current information on the services available to you, ask a librarian for assistance.

Commercial Services

In previous chapters, we have mentioned that some publishers of indexes and abstracting services provide document-delivery services for a fee. Some of these are offered by federal government or quasigovernmental agencies: the Government Printing Office, the ERIC Document Reproduction Service, and the National Technical Information Service. Others are provided by commercial publishers of indexes: the Genuine Article™ service for *Current Contents* and copies of dissertations from University Microfilms International.

Another option, if you cannot or do not want to use ILL or to travel, is employing an organization that provides copies of documents and articles as a business. An advantage of this option is speed. Some companies accept telephone requests, rush requests, and credit-card payment for services. Some companies specialize in particular subject areas or in rare documents. You can get the names and addresses of these organizations from directories such as the biennial *Document Retrieval: Sources and Services* and the annual *Directory of Fee-Based Information Services.* The primary disadvantage of these sources, however, is cost: These services are very expensive. To obtain a single journal article may cost you $10 or more, not including special services such as rush delivery. Therefore, you must address the issues of how badly you need the information and how much it is worth to you.

References

American Psychiatric Association. (1987). *Diagnostic and statistical manual of mental disorders* (3rd ed., rev.). Washington, DC: Author.

Biederman, J., Munir, K., Knee, D., Habelow, W., Armentano, M., Autor, S., Hoge, S. K., & Waternaux, C. (1986). A family study of patients with Attention Deficit Disorder and normal controls. *Journal of Psychiatric Research, 20,* 263–274.

Broadbent, D. E. (1958). *Perception and communication.* New York: Pergamon Press.

Cherry, E. C. (1953). Some experiments on the recognition of speech, with one and two ears. *Journal of the Acoustical Society of America, 25,* 975–979.

CRM. (1971). *Information processing* [Film]. Del Mar, CA: CRM/McGraw-Hill Films.

Crooks, R. L., & Stein, J. (1988). *Psychology: Science, behavior and life.* New York: Holt, Rinehart & Winston.

Directory of fee-based information services. (1990–present). Houston, TX: Burwell Enterprises.

Document retrieval: Sources and services. (1981–present). San Francisco: The Information Store.

Henker, B., & Whalen, C. K. (1989). Hyperactivity and attention deficits. *American Psychologist, 44,* 216–223.

Johnston, W. A., & Dark, V. J. (1986). Selective attention. *Annual Review of Psychology, 37,* 43–75.

MacLeod, C. M. (1991). Half a century of research on the Stroop effect: An integrative review. *Psychological Bulletin, 109,* 163–203.

Matlin, M. W. (1983). *Perception.* Boston: Allyn & Bacon.

Shiffrin, R. M. (1986). Attention. In R. C. Atlinson, R. J. Herrnstein, G. Lindzey, & R. D. Luce (Eds.), *Stevens' handbook of experimental psychology: Volume 2. Learning and cognition* (2nd ed., pp. 739–811). New York: Wiley.

Stroop, J. R. (1935). Studies of interference in serial verbal reactions. *Journal of Experimental Psychology, 18,* 643–662.

Zametkin, A. J., Nordahl, T. E., Gross, M., King, A. C., Semple, W. E., Rumsey, J., Hamburger, S., & Cohen, R. M. (1990). Cerebral glucose metabolism in adults with hyperactivity of childhood onset. *The New England Journal of Medicine, 323,* 1361–1366.

Appendixes

A: Additional Specialized Sources
B: Brief Guide to Literature Searching
C: Exercises and Other Topics to Pursue

Appendix A: Additional Specialized Sources

This appendix lists and annotates a variety of sources not discussed within the book. This is a selected list; that is, we have not attempted to be inclusive but have tried to illustrate the various types of sources available. Some sources are very specialized and, therefore, may not be available in your library. Other sources may be primarily of interest to teachers and researchers rather than to students. If you are interested in further information or in additional sources, consult McInnis (1982).

Psychology Bibliographies

McInnis, R. G. (1982). *Research guide for psychology.* Westport, CT: Greenwood Press.

In more than 580 pages, this work lists and describes more than 1,200 bibliographic sources in psychology.

Watson, R. I., Sr. (Ed.). (1974). *Eminent contributors to psychology* (2 vols.). New York: Springer. *Volume 1: A bibliography of primary references. Volume 2: A bibliography of secondary references.*

This reference tool is especially useful for the history of psychology.

Dictionaries and Encyclopedias

The following sources are useful in providing brief definitions and short articles. These books supplement handbooks mentioned in chapter 2.

American handbook of psychiatry (2nd ed., 8 vols.) (1974–1986). New York: Basic Books.

Corsini, R. J. (Ed.). (1984). *Encyclopedia of psychology* (Vols. 1–4). New York: Wiley.

Harre, R., & Lamb, R. (Eds.). (1983). *Encyclopedic dictionary of psychology.* Cambridge, MA: MIT Press.

International encyclopedia of the social sciences (18 vols.). (1968). New York: Macmillan.

Koch, S. (Ed.). (1959–1963). *Psychology: A study of a science* (6 vols.). New York: McGraw-Hill

Produced with the support of the American Psychological Association and the National Science Foundation, this series explores the foundations and the development of psychology and the relationship of psychology to other sciences.

Stratton, P., & Hayes, N. (1988). *A student's dictionary of psychology.* London: Edward Arnold.

Wolman, B. B. (Ed.). (1977). *International encyclopedia of psychiatry, psychology, psychoanalysis and neurology* (12 vols.). New York: Van Nostrand Reinhold for Aesculapius Press.

Progress Volume I. (1983). New York: Aesculapius Publishers.

Wolman, B. B. (Ed.). (1989). *Dictionary of behavioral science* (2nd ed.). New York: Academic.

Statistics Handbooks

Andrews, F. M., Klem, L., Davidson, T. M., O'Malley, P. M., & Rodgers, W. L. (1981). *A guide for selecting statistical techniques for analyzing social science data* (2nd ed.). Ann Arbor, MI: Survey Research Center, University of Michigan.

Beyer, W. H. (Compiler). (1968). *CRC handbook of tables for probability and statistics* (2nd ed.). Cleveland: Chemical Rubber Co.

Burington, R. S., & May, D. C. (1970). *Handbook of probability and statistics with tables* (2nd ed.). New York: McGraw-Hill.

Yaremko, R. M., Harari, H., Harrison, R. C., & Lynn, E. (1982). *Reference handbook of research and statistical methods in psychology: For students and professionals.* New York: Harper & Row.

Directories

The following may be primarily of interest to researchers and faculty members. Use these sources with caution because the information may change quickly.

American Psychological Association. (1987). *Guide to research support* (3rd ed.). Washington, DC: Author.

Annual register of grant support. (1969–present). Chicago: Marquis. Annual.

Bauer, D. G. (1985). *Complete grants sourcebook for higher education* (2nd ed.). New York: American Council on Education.

Encyclopedia of associations. (1956–present). Detroit, MI: Gale. Annual.

Foundation directory. (1960–present). New York: Foundation Center. Biennial.

Research centers directory (15th ed.). (1965–present). Detroit, MI: Gale. Annual.

Guides to Journals

Useful in deciding where to submit a manuscript, these guides include information about editorial policies of journals, acceptance rates, publication lag, and so forth. Information becomes dated quickly in this area, so use these sources with care.

Journals in psychology: A resource listing for authors (3rd ed.). (1990). Washington, DC: American Psychological Association.

Wang, A. Y. (1989). *Author's guide to journals in the behavioral sciences.* Hillsdale, NJ: Lawrence Erlbaum.

Indexes and Abstracts

Some of the following specialized services may be extremely useful. Because of their limited scope and the expense involved in subscribing to many possibly overlapping sources, however, these services may not be available through your library.

Animal behaviour abstracts. (1973–present). London: Information Retrieval Ltd. Quarterly.

Child development abstracts and bibliography. (1927–present). Chicago: University of Chicago Press. Three times a year.

Criminal justice abstracts. (1969–present). Monsey, NY: Willow Tree Press. Quarterly. (Formerly published by the National Council on Crime and Delinquency Information Center.)

Criminal justice periodical index. (1975–present). Ann Arbor, MI: University Microfilms International. Annual.

Criminology and penology abstracts. (1961–present). Amsterdam: Kugler. Bimonthly. (Formerly: *Abstracts on criminology and penology* and *Excerpta criminologica.*)

Ergonomics abstracts. (1969–present). London: Taylor & Francis. Bimonthly.

Excerpta medica: Section 32. Psychiatry. (1948–present). Amsterdam: Excerpta Medica. Twenty times a year.

Excerpta medica: Section 40. Drug dependence. (1973–present). Amsterdam: Excerpta Medica. Monthly.

Index to current urban documents. (1972/1973–present). Westport, CT: Greenwood. Quarterly.

> This index covers publications issued by major American and Canadian cities and counties.

Index to periodical articles by and about Blacks. (1973–present). Boston: G. K. Hall. Annual. (Formerly: *Index to periodical articles by and about Negroes,* 1950–1972.)

L'année psychologique. (1894–present). Paris: Presses Universitaires de France. Semiannual.

Linguistics and language behavior abstracts. (1967–present). LaJolla, CA: Sociological Abstracts. Quarterly.

Personnel literature (1941–present). Washington, DC: U.S. Office of Personnel Management. Monthly. (Formerly issued by the U.S. Civil Service Commission Library.)

Women studies abstacts. (1972–present). Rush, NY: Rush Publishing. Quarterly.

General Bibliographies

You can use the following sources to check on the current availability of books.

Books in print. (1948–present). New York: Bowker. Annual.

Forthcoming books. (1966–present). New York: Bowker. Bimonthly.

Publisher's trade list annual. (1872–present). New York: Bowker. Annual.

Subject guide to books in print. (1957–present). New York: Bowker. Annual.

Supplement to Books in Print. (1971/1973–present). New York: Bowker. Annual.

National Bibliographies

You will find that the primary function the following sources serve is verification of the accuracy of bibliographic information about a particular source. They attempt to be inclusive, covering most materials published and copyrighted in the United States or held by American libraries. The lists for books and serials are listed below chronologically by years of coverage.

Books

National union catalog, pre-1956 imprints (685 vols.). (1967–1980). London: Mansell. *Supplement* (69 vols.). (1980–1981).

Library of Congress catalog. Books: Subjects; A cumulative list of works represented by Library of Congress printed cards. [1950–1954 (20 vols.); 1955–1959 (22 vols.); 1960–1964 (25 vols.); 1965–1969 (42 vols.); 1970–1974 (100 vols.)] (Publisher varies). (Continued by Library of Congress *Subject Catalog.*)

National union catalog: A cumulative author list representing Library of Congress printed cards and titles reported by other American libraries. (1956–1978). Washington, DC: Library of Congress. [1953–1957 (26 vols.); 1958–1962 (50 vols.); 1963–1967 (59 vols.); 1968–1972 (104 vols.); 1973–1977 (135 vols.)]. (Publisher varies.)

National union catalog. (1979–1983). Washington, DC: Library of Congress. (Continued by *NUC: Books.*)

Library of Congress. (1975–1982). *Subject catalog.* Washington, DC: Author. (Continued by *NUC: Books.*)

NUC: Books. (1983–present). Washington, DC: Library of Congress.

Published monthly in microfiche and cumulated annually and quinquenially (1983–1987). The register section provides complete information on all books cataloged by the Library of Congress (and some other libraries up to 1991). Access to the register is by name, title, Library of Congress subject heading, and series indexes.

Serials

Union list of serials in libraries of the United States and Canada (3rd ed., 5 vols.). (1965). New York: H. W. Wilson.

New serial titles: A union list of serials commencing publication after December 31, 1949. (1953–present). Washington, DC: Library of Congress. Monthly. *1950–1970 Cumulative* (4 vols.). (1973). *1971–1975 Cumulation* (2 vols.). (1976). *1976–1980 Cumulation* (2 vols.). (1981). *1981–1985 Cumulation* (6 vols.). (1986). *1986–1989 Cumulation* (6 vols.). (1990).

New serial titles: Classed subject arrangement. (1955–present). Washington, DC: Library of Congress. Monthly.

OCLC [Machine-readable bibliographic file]. (1967–present). Dublin, OH: OCLC.

OCLC is a database composed of over 20 million records representing books, journals, manuscripts, and audiovisual materials held by over 4,000 libraries, most American. In addition to bibliographic information, each record is accompanied by location codes indicating the libraries holding that title.

RLIN [Machine-readable bibliographic file]. (1974–present). Stanford, CA: Research Libraries Group.

Similar to OCLC, RLIN (Research Libraries Information Network) represents holdings from approximately 50 major research libraries in the United States.

Appendix B: Brief Guide to Literature Searching

The step-by-step guidelines provided below will help you organize and conduct a literature search. Complete each section in sequential order. Record actual sources located in the search on individual index cards as suggested in chapter 1. In parentheses are the chapters in which particular steps in the process and bibliographic resources are discussed.

Stage 1: Defining and Limiting the Topic (chapter 2)
- State the general topic.
- Briefly define the topic.
- Provide an initial source or reference.
- Find a review source for general background:
  Textbook
  Annual review
  Handbook
- Limit the topic by one or more of the following:
  Subarea
  Theory
  Species
  Research methodology
  Time period
  Other
- State the narrowed topic statement or research question.
- Are there further possibilities for limitation? What are these?
- Ask self-analyzing questions:
  What do you find most interesting about this topic?
  Why are you interested in this area?
- State the narrowed topic.
- List original primary sources (journal articles, authors, etc.).
- List subject-search terms.

Stage 2: Finding Books (chapters 3 and 4)
For a general overview and possible important new contributions to the topic area, take these steps:

- List important authors and titles to consult.
- List subject headings for the card or online catalog.
- *PsycBOOKS*

Stage 3: Finding Research in Journal Articles With a Subject Search (chapters 4 and 5)
- List the sources to be consulted (depending on area).
  Psychological Abstracts
  ERIC *Current Index to Journals in Education* and *Resources in Education* or *Education Index*
  Business Periodicals Index
  Sociological Abstracts
  Index Medicus
  Others (see Appendix A)

- Consult a thesaurus (if available). List acceptable subject headings for the topic. (Modify the list, as needed, while conducting the search.)
- List bibliographic sources consulted.

Stage 4: Searching by Author/Citation in Addition to or Instead of by Subject (chapter 6)

Answer the following questions. If you answer "yes" to each, proceed using *Social Sciences Citation Index.* If you answer "no" to the questions, a citation search will not be helpful.

- Do you have access to *SSCI?*
- Do you have an important initial reference critical to early development of the field? If "yes," what is the reference?

Stage 5: Locating Relevant Government Documents (chapter 7)

Ask yourself whether this is an area in which governmental agencies have an interest. If "yes," then:

- Check the *Monthly Catalog.*
- Check the *Index to U.S. Government Periodicals.*

Stage 6: Considering a Computer Search (chapter 8)

Before initiating a search, consider the following questions:

- Is this service available to you?
- Is there a charge involved? If so, how much?
- Is the search worth doing?
- Do you know enough about the topic to formulate a specific query?

If you decide to proceed, do the following:

- Find out who to contact for a search conducted by a librarian or if your library has CD-ROM indexes.
- Decide which databases should be searched.
- Prepare a search strategy, including all of the information gathered in Stages 1 and 3 above.
- If using CD-ROM, review instructional material on the service.

Stage 7: Locating Materials Not in the Library (chapter 11)

Before requesting interlibrary loan services, ascertain the following:

- Is interlibrary loan service available to you?
- Which unavailable materials do you really need?
- Is there a charge for the service? If so, how much?
- How long will you have to wait for the materials?
- Are you able to travel to use other library collections?

If able to proceed based on the answers to questions, then do the following:

- Record complete and accurate bibliographic information on each source you request.
- Keep a record of each source request.
- Ask if, when, and how you will be notified about receipt of the materials.

Appendix C: Exercises and Other Topics to Pursue

The purpose of this appendix is twofold. It can provide students with research topic ideas. For instructors, it may provide exercises to help students learn more about library research.

Background

In writing this book, we considered a large number of topics for use as chapter examples to illustrate searches with the tools we covered. We have used topics from many areas in the field of psychology. We established a variety of criteria for topic inclusion. Topics had to be:

* **Interesting.** The topic should be of a general interest to many undergraduate psychology students.
* **Accessible.** Information on the topic should be available in a typical college library.
* **Reported.** There must be a body of published research available on the topic.
* **Covered.** The topic must be available in the literature covered by the source.
* **Current.** It must be a topic of interest to students today.
* **General.** The topic must not be so technical that few students will have the background to understand or pursue the topic.
* **Mainline.** The topic must be within the domain of generally acceptable psychological inquiry. We attempted to avoid fads and fringe topics.

Because of the length of the book, we were able to use only a few of the topics we explored. The topics listed below are some of those that we investigated but did not use. For each topic, we have provided a very brief introduction and a few key sources. The sources are not always the most critical or most relevant, but are those that we have found interesting.

Use the information contained in this book and summarized in Appendix B to structure and conduct a literature search on a topic from the list below.

Sample Topics

Amnesia and the Neuropsychology of Memory

There are several types of amnesia. Disease-induced amnesia may result from problems such as stroke or Alzheimer's disease. In a severe case, it can be indicative of widespread brain degeneration and reflect significant memory loss. Retrograde amnesia, frequently resulting from head injury, is a loss of memory for information or events prior to the injury. Anterograde amnesia is the loss of memory for information or events following an injury. Research has linked certain types of amnesia to lesions in particular areas of the brain; for example, retrograde amnesia has been linked to medial temporal lesions. What can we learn about human memory through studying amnesia? How are brain mechanisms different for different amnesia types?

Schacter, D. L. (1987). Memory, amnesia, and frontal lobe dysfunction. *Psychobiology, 15,* 21–36.

Shimamura, A. P., & Squire, L. R. (1987). Neuropsychological study of fact memory and source amnesia. *Journal of Experimental Psychology: Learning, Memory, and Cognition, 13,* 464–473.

Squire, L. R. (1986, June 27). Mechanisms of memory. *Science, 232,* 1612–1619.

Squire, L. R., & Frambach, M. (1990). Cognitive skill learning in amnesia. *Psychobiology, 18,* 109–117.

Squire, L. R., & Butters, N. (Eds.). (1984). *Neuropsychology of memory.* New York: Guilford Press.

Children's Work

Children in many families regularly perform household tasks (e.g., taking out the garbage, washing dishes, or feeding pets). Tasks appear to differ relative to variables such as age of the child, socioeconomic status, and location (rural versus urban). Task performance is frequently linked to rewards (an "allowance"). To what extent does childhood work support learning, positive work values, and socialization?

Goodnow, J. J. (1988). Children's household work: Its nature and functions. *Psychological Bulletin, 103,* 5–26.

White, L. K., & Brinkerhoff, D. B. (1981). Children's work in the family: Its significance and meaning. *Journal of Marriage and the Family, 43,* 789–798.

Evolution and Psychology

The past few centuries have seen remarkable changes in technology, health care, and government. Biological changes within the human organism cannot be said to have occurred at such a furious pace. Yet, changes in the world have had a significant and enduring impact on human behavior. We have adapted in areas such as work, family, sex roles, and social behavior. Most of these social and psychological changes have been evolutionary in nature. How can an understanding of evolution help provide better psychological theories of behavior?

Crawford, C. B. (1989). The theory of evolution: Of what value to psychology? *Journal of Comparative Psychology, 103,* 4–22.

Trivers, R. L. (1985). *Social evolution.* Menlo Park, CA: Benjamin/Cummings.

Groupthink

Groups sometimes develop a climate in which cohesiveness, consensus-seeking, and unanimity become so important that a premium is placed on avoiding conflict. The tendency in such groups is to place a negative value on independent critical thinking and to avoid asking difficult questions. Such groups have been known to make flawed decisions because they failed to evaluate potentially negative aspects of a course of action. Examples of government groupthink include the Bay of Pigs invasion, the surprise attack on Pearl Harbor, and the Korean War escalation. How can one recognize groupthink in the workplace and what can be done to prevent it?

Callaway, M. R., & Esser, J. K. (1984). Groupthink: Effects of cohesiveness and problem-solving procedures on group decision making. *Social Behavior and Personality, 12,* 157–164.

Esser, J. K., & Lindoerfer, J. S. (1989). Groupthink and the space shuttle Challenger accident: Toward a quantitative case analysis. *Journal of Behavioral Decision Making, 2,* 167–177.

Janis, I. L. (1982). *Groupthink: Psychological studies of policy decisions and fiascoes* (2nd ed.). Boston: Houghton Mifflin.

Tetlock. P. E. (1979). Identifying victims of groupthink from public statements of decision makers. *Journal of Personality and Social Psychology, 37,* 1314–1324.

Learned Helplessness

This condition occurs when an individual believes that it is impossible to escape or avoid aversive events. It occurs as a result of prior exposure to inescapable aversive stimulation. Learned helplessness appears to impair the ability to learn. The phenomenon was initially demonstrated in dogs subjected to electrical shock and has been extended to other species, including humans, in many situations. What relevance does learned helplessness have to our everyday life?

Kofta, M., & Sedek, G. (1989). Repeated failure: A source of helplessness or a factor irrelevant to its emergence? *Journal of Experimental Psychology: General, 118,* 3–12.

Seligman, M. E. (1975). *Helplessness: On depression, development, and death.* San Francisco, CA: W. H. Freeman.

Seligman, M. E., & Maier, S. F. (1967). Failure to escape traumatic shock. *Journal of Experimental Psychology, 74,* 1–9.

Winefield, A. H. (1982). Methodological difficulties in demonstrating learned helplessness in humans. *Journal of General Psychology, 107,* 255–266.

Multiple Memory Systems

Researchers have provided evidence for procedural memory (that which enables learning of stimulus–response contingencies), semantic memory (the ability to internally represent the world), and episodic memory (an ability to comprehend experiences and time). How many memory systems are there? What is the relationship among such memory systems?

Humphreys, M. S., Bain, J. D., & Pike, R. (1989). Different ways to cue a coherent memory system: A theory for episodic, semantic, and procedural tasks. *Psychological Review, 96,* 208–233.

Mitchell, D. B. (1989). How many memory systems? Evidence from aging. *Journal of Experimental Psychology: Learning, Memory, and Cognition, 15,* 31–49.

Tulving, E. (1985). How many memory systems are there? *American Psychologist, 40,* 385–398.

Obedience

In a now classic series of studies, Stanley Milgram was able to demonstrate that individuals will punish others (through administration of electric shocks as punishment for learning errors) at the direction of an authority figure, even when such punishment may not seem reasonable. To what extent and under what conditions can individuals be expected to conform to directions from individuals perceived as authorities?

Milgram, S. (1963). Behavioral study of obedience. *Journal of Abnormal Psychology, 67*, 371–378.

Milgram, S. (1974). *Obedience to authority: An experimental view.* New York: Harper & Row.

Sabini, J., & Silver, M. (1983). Dispositional vs. situational interpretations of Milgram's obedience experiment: "The fundamental attributional error." *Journal for the Theory of Social Behavior, 13*, 147–154.

Shanab, M. E., & Yahya, K. A. (1977). A behavioral study of obedience in children. *Journal of Personality and Social Psychology, 35*, 530–536.

Pavlovian Conditioning

Understanding of Pavlovian conditioning has changed significantly in the past few decades. Once described as the simple pairing or contingency of events, it is becoming increasingly clear that there is a need for the organism to learn about relationships among events. Additionally, two-process theory has noted a much closer link between Pavlovian conditioning and instrumental learning than was thought to be the case in previous decades. What is the current understanding of Pavlovian conditioning, and in dealing with what areas of behavior is this important?

Rescorla, R. A. (1988). Pavlovian conditioning: It's not what you think it is. *American Psychologist, 43*, 152–160.

Rescorla, R. A., & Solomon, R. L. (1967). Two-process learning theory: Relationships between Pavlovian conditioning and instrumental learning. *Psychological Review, 74*, 152–182.

Primary Prevention in the Schools

The goal of primary prevention is to develop programs to deter psychological problems and to build support for psychological well-being. Both system-centered and person-centered approaches have been taken. Primary prevention mechanisms have included changing the social environment, early childhood stimulation, and primary mental health. A significant effort has been the primary mental health project in the schools. How successful is primary prevention?

Cowen, E. L. (1984). A general structural model for primary prevention program development in mental health. *Personnel and Guidance Journal, 62*, 485–490.

Cowen, E. L. (1986). Primary prevention in mental health: A decade of retrospect and a decade of prospect. In M. Kessler & S. Goldston (Eds.), *Decade of progress in primary prevention* (pp. 3–45). Hanover, NH: University Press of New England.

Cowen, E. L., & Hightower, A. D. (1990). The Primary Mental Health Project: Alternative approaches in school-based preventive intervention. In T. B. Gutkin & C. R. Reynolds (Eds.), *Handbook of school psychology* (2nd ed., pp. 775–795). New York: John Wiley.

Sensitive Periods

At particular points in the life cycle, organisms appear to be especially sensitive to learning as a result of external experiences. Exposure, or lack of exposure, to particular events during a sensitive period can have a significant impact on the individual's subsequent behavior. Reported instances of such critical periods include imprinting in ducks, language acquisition in children, and emotionality in monkeys. For what types of human behavioral development are sensitive periods important?

Bornstein, M. H. (1987). *Sensitive periods in development: Interdisciplinary perspectives.* Hillsdale, NJ: Lawrence Erlbaum.

Bornstein, M. H. (1989). Sensitive periods in development: Structural characteristics and causal interpretations. *Psychological Bulletin, 105,* 179–197.

Teacher Expectations (Pygmalion Effect)

Teachers exert a tremendous amount of influence on student performance in a classroom setting. Subtle, as well as blatant, influences by a teacher can have a profound effect on helping children with difficulties to do well or discouraging gifted and promising children. The Pygmalion effect has been noted in the context of school performance of minority or disadvantaged children. What can teachers do to avoid the problem of the Pygmalion effect when it is destructive of child learning?

Jussim, L. (1989). Teacher expectations: Self-fulfilling prophecies, perceptual biases, and accuracy. *Journal of Personality and Social Psychology, 57,* 469–480.

Rosenthal, R., & Jacobson, L. (1968). *Pygmalion in the classroom: Teacher expectation and pupils' intellectual development.* New York: Holt, Rinehart & Winston.

Treatment Effectiveness With Bipolar Disorders

Psychological treatment of bipolar disorders (manic-depression) may encompass a variety of approaches: individual psychotherapy, group psychotherapy, behavior therapy, marital therapy, cognitive–behavior therapy, social learning therapy, pharmacotherapy, and electroconvulsive shock therapy. Effectiveness varies depending on such factors as problem severity, therapeutic approach, and therapist characteristics. What approaches have been most effective under what conditions for the treatment of depression?

Beckham, E. E. (1984). The comparative efficacy of psychotherapy and pharmacotherapy in depression: Implications for clinical practice. *Psychotherapy in Private Practice, 2,* 31–37.

Steinbrueck, S. M., Maxwell, S. E., & Howard, G. S. (1983). A meta-analysis of psychotherapy and drug therapy in the treatment of unipolar depression with adults. *Journal of Consulting and Clinical Psychology, 51,* 856–863.

Teri, L., & Lewinsohn, P. M. (1986). Individual and group treatment of unipolar depression: Comparison of treatment outcome and identification of predictors of successful treatment outcome. *Behavior Therapy, 17,* 215–228.

Vocational Interest Tests

Interest inventories are often used in career counseling. They attempt to match an individual's profile of responses to a standard series of questions with profiles of typical occupational incumbents to develop a vocational interest profile for the individual.

One of the more popular and widely used vocational interest inventories is the Strong Interest Inventory (previously published as the Strong Vocational Interest Blank and as the Strong-Campbell Interest Inventory). This test was most recently revised in 1985.

Having identified the Strong Interest Inventory, before using it, we need to learn about it. In addition to examining the manual, we should also consult general information about vocational choices and careers, as well as evaluative information about this particular measurement instrument.

Holland, J. L. (1985). *Making vocational choices: A theory of vocational personalities and work environments* (2nd ed.). Englewood Cliffs, NJ: Prentice-Hall.

Layton, W. L. (1985). [Review of *Strong-Campbell Interest Inventory*]. In J. V. Mitchell, Jr. (Ed.), *Ninth Mental Measurements Yearbook* (Vol. II, pp. 1480–1481). Lincoln, NE: Buros Institute of Mental Measurements, University of Nebraska-Lincoln.

London, M., & Stumpf, S. A. (1982) *Managing careers.* Reading, MA: Addison Wesley.

Strong, E. K., Hansen, J. C. & Campbell, D. P. (1985). *Strong interest inventory.* Palo Alto, CA: Consulting Psychologists Press.

Westbrook, B. W. (1985). [Review of *Strong-Campbell Interest Inventory*]. In J. V. Mitchell, Jr. (Ed.), *Ninth Mental Measurements Yearbook* (Vol. II, pp. 1481–1483). Lincoln, NE: Buros Institute of Mental Measurements, University of Nebraska.

Women in Management

Social changes have allowed an increasing number of women to assume positions of significant managerial responsibility and authority in business, governmental, and social organizations. Do the experiences of men and women in senior management positions differ? Do men and women differ in their success in managerial roles? How have women managers handled cultural expectations and stereotypes regarding marriage, children, career, and mobility?

Adler, N. J., & Izraeli, D. N. (Eds.). (1988). *Women in management worldwide.* Armonk, NY: M. E. Sharpe.

Freeman, S. J. M. (1990). *Managing lives: Corporate women and social change.* Amherst, MA: University of Massachusetts Press.

Morrison, A. M., & Von Glinow, M. A. (1990). Women and minorities in management. *American Psychologist, 45,* 200–208.

Powell, G. N. (1988). *Women and men in management.* Newbury Park, CA: Sage Publications.

Index

About the Authors

Jeffrey G. Reed is software program manager at Xerox Corporation. He has also worked as assistant professor of psychology at SUNY–Geneseo; assistant reference librarian at Bucknell University; organizational and training consultant in Rochester, NY; user interface software design manager and user interface software developer at Xerox Corporation; and educational researcher at Kansas State University and Towson State University. He has conducted research on motivation, satisfaction, academic performance, teaching effectiveness, human–computer interaction, and library use, with articles in journals such as *Journal of Educational Psychology, Teaching of Psychology, Research in Higher Education,* and *Measurement and Evaluation in Guidance.*

Pam M. Baxter is head of the Psychological Sciences Library and associate professor of library science at Purdue University. She was previously reference librarian at SUNY–Geneseo and bibliographer for the Self-Assessment for Colleges and Universities Project, New York State Department of Education. She has written on bibliographic instruction, with emphasis on the information gathering skills of and literature search methods employed by psychologists and psychology students.